I0192030

Dr. Gao brings us advanced knowledge of investment, financial management, and economics from his learning. He also guides us and encourages us through his detours and experiences. I learned a lot from reading this book. In Dr. Gao's view, everyone has the potential to achieve success. He believes everyone has the opportunity to be rich.

Dr. Kimball K.H.Au Yeung
Author of **Your Key To Harvard**

Readers of this book will enjoy the vignettes of Dr. Gao's incredibly interesting life and will learn from his acquired knowledge of investing. His powerful story of success is based on the premise that everyone has the potential to achieve financial success if they can take advantage of the opportunities in life that can make anyone wealthy.

Dr. William Chappell
Associate Professor of Economics
University of Mississippi

This book made me think about what kind of life I want. It encouraged me to never give up. In many people's view, Dr. Gao has a successful life now. But during his journey on the road to success, he made a lot of detours. He also experienced confusion like many of us. Now he writes this book to share his experiences and lessons to help people create a vision for their ideal life and fight for it. Even though, in others' eyes, Dr. Gao is already a successful man, he does not slack off. He is just like an adventurer who is using his full energy to unceasingly challenge higher mountains and pursue his goals for life.

Mengqiu Guo
Zhengzhou, China

Secrets from My Money-Smart BROTHER

Modern Strategies for Attaining Wealth, Health, and Happiness

知识创造财富

Hongman Gao, PhD

Soar with Eagles

A Publisher Driven
by Vision and Purpose
www.soarhigher.com

Secrets from My Money-Smart Brother:
Modern Strategies for Attaining
Wealth, Health, and Happiness

Copyright © 2011 by Hongman Gao, PhD. All rights reserved.

ISBN-13: 978-0-9814756-8-4
Library of Congress Control Number 2011930646

No part of this book may be reproduced, stored in a retrieval system, or transmitted in any form or by any means — electronic, mechanical, photocopy, recording, or any other except for the inclusion of brief quotations in a review — without written permission from Soar with Eagles.

First Edition

Published by
Soar with Eagles
2809 Laurel Crossing, Rogers, AR 72758 USA
 www.soarhigher.com

Design and editing by Carrie Perrien Smith

Printed in the United States of America

Contents

智慧

智慧

Introduction

It Does Not Matter How You Start

"There are two things to aim at in life:
first to get what you want; and, after that, to enjoy it."
Logan Pearsall Smith

My family lived in a mountainous area in eastern China. I have six brothers and three sisters, and I am the youngest. My father died when I was four years old. It left my mother to raise ten children by herself. Life wasn't ever easy for my family, but it became even harder when my father died.

In 1970s, it was especially tough. Sometimes we had nothing to eat. My mother had to go to the mountains to pick up tree leaves and dig up tree roots to feed us. Later on, the government gave us a little piece of private land so we could produce some of our own food. Part of the road to my home was very steep. It was long walk too — more than 360 steps. The only way to get to it was on foot.

We chopped bamboo to sell. We would carry the bamboo ten miles down the mountains to flatter terrain. Then, we transported it by cart to a small town twenty-five miles away to sell. It provided money we needed to buy rice and meat for our family.

Our schools were shabby, broken-down buildings. I walked seven miles to my elementary school. It was a fifteen-mile walk to my middle school. My high school was twenty-five miles from home.

Although our family was poor, we all felt optimistic. We never quarreled about money. We knew we all had to pitch in and help bring money into the household for the things we needed. In middle school, I needed money to buy new shoes and socks. I went to work selling wood I cut from the mountain near my home. I even took my brother with me.

I developed a good relationship with the company who bought my wood. I was the first person in my school to successfully negotiate with them. My work helped my classmates because it paved the way for some of them to sell wood to the same company. I eventually moved on to start another business. I knew running a business would mean I wouldn't have the time to work as hard in school. However, I could make money our family badly needed.

Our family was poor, but we each were allowed to keep some of the money we earned. I would buy my mother something she enjoyed, such as apples. She was so grateful, but she would have really been mad if she knew I was concentrating on earning money instead of studying.

When I was in middle school, we didn't have a clock. We had to look at the stars and the moon to tell the time. If it was rainy or foggy or the moonlight was gone, we couldn't tell what time it was.

I would normally get up around 5:30 a.m. to make it to school by 8:00 a.m. Some days, we had to carry fifty kilos of wood before school. We would get up around midnight on those days just to make sure we had enough time.

I was very timid as a child. The adults would tell ghost stories for entertainment. I always listened intently, but it made me so afraid of the dark. My mother locked the door behind me when I set off for school each morning before dawn. All I could think of was the ghosts lurking behind every tree.

I just kept going and never looked back. I never told my mother how afraid I was. I didn't want her to feel bad because her son was scared to walk alone in the dark. I figured I should be brave enough to solve my own problems. Besides, the wood on my shoulder was heavy. Turning around to look back at my mom would only prolong the journey to town. I knew my mom would cry if she saw her son struggling. I would do anything to make my mother happy. She was the real reason I worked and studied hard.

Among my brothers and sisters, two brothers are very different from the other siblings. Both had their own strong viewpoints on financial situations. Both placed an emphasis on education, but one focused on school education and degree learning. The other emphasized lifelong learning and knowledge application.

The one who emphasized knowledge application found a passion in obtaining useful knowledge. He finished his undergraduate and graduate degrees and finally earned a PhD. Let's call him my money-smart brother.

The other focused on book learning and degree education. He got bored, never found his area of interest, and ended up terminating his education after earning his high school degree. We'll call him my money-dumb brother.

When we experienced financial crises, my money-dumb brother suggested we needed to wait for the government to help. He assured us the government would take care of everything and we did not need to do anything. My money-smart brother provided wise advice and suggested we take action in order to survive. He was skeptical the government would help us. He believed we needed to take charge of our destiny. At the time, I was young. These different opinions confused me. But the more I listened to their arguments, the more I learned important lessons for my life.

My money-smart brother always told me that I should work doing something I loved to do. He said the money would follow my passion. He believed if you found something interesting, you would put your whole heart into it. My money-dumb brother told me we needed to work for money. He said we should go where we could earn money. It did not matter where your interests were; as long as you could earn money, you would always feel good.

Their differing opinions didn't stop with just work. My money-dumb brother always said that money was evil and rich people were greedy. On the other hand, my money-smart brother said that money was good but the love of money was the root of all evil. When economic times were not good, my money-dumb brother would say we shouldn't invest our money because the economy was bad and the stock market had crashed. My money-smart brother would say that a tough economy was the best time to invest because the economic fundamentals were sound and the price of stocks and mutual funds were so low.

Their differing viewpoints led them to follow different paths in life. The money-smart brother chose to seek educational opportunities and ultimately earn his PhD. He became rich. He was a self-made millionaire by the time he was twenty-seven years old. My money-dumb brother stayed at home, focused on the government and politics, and became broke. He retired in a very poor financial condition.

I began learning lessons from my brothers when I was very young. Watching both of them affected my thinking and eventually impacted my life. I consider myself fortunate to grow up in an environment with various perspectives. When I listened to my money-smart brother, I learned his knowledge and wisdom. However, upon listening to my money-dumb brother, I realized that his bad ideas and opinions could affect my way of thinking and negatively impact my life. The more I listened and learned, the more I agreed with my money-smart brother's opinions.

Because of their different views, I began to change my way of thinking as I grew older. I realized along the way that I had the ability to do and learn whatever I wanted and needed. Of course, I encountered many barriers and roadblocks on my education, career, and investing paths. Life is not meant to be easy because we learn by solving problems! But as I experienced tough situations, I always remembered my brothers' lessons.

Even with their knowledge and experience, I learned my own lessons and gained my own experience. I realized that managing money was a skill and achieving financial independence should be one of your first goals in life. But besides achieving financial freedom, you should also achieve your life's goals with physical, mental, and spiritual freedom.

Both of my brothers taught me that education was the key to success, but my money-smart brother advised me to become a lifelong learner. This particular lesson lives in my heart. When I finished college, I went to work for the government. For five years, my job was to supervise the financial industry. I returned to school for three years to finish my first master's degree. Once I completed my degree, I returned to work for the government for one year to supervise the stock market. I decided it was time to come to the United States to continue my learning, so I quit my job. I went on to finish two more master's degrees and my PhD in the United States.

I also learned some of my life lessons in business. One summer during junior high, I bought some necessities in town to sell for a small profit to people living in the remote mountain area. When I worked for the government, I started a small business with my friends where we rented bicycles to travelers. The bicycle rental business eventually failed because all the bicycles were stolen.

My brothers' lessons about saving and investing inspired me to start investing in stocks. I began to invest after I got my first job. I failed at first because I paid too much attention to bad news. I worried too much about the bad economy and stock market crashes. But through all the lessons and mistakes, I've learned to save and invest properly.

Based on my two brothers' lessons and my own experience, I found an investing system that never fails — even in a financial crisis. It uses an automatic system to save and invest regularly based on dollar cost average investing, and it doesn't matter whether the stock market is good or bad. Through it, I'm able to achieve the stock market average growth. In more than 100 years, the U.S. stock market growth has averaged 10 to 12 percent.

I learned from my brothers that I should not only work hard, but also work smart. Because most of us are working-class people, we always need to improve our knowledge and value. It enables us to contribute more to our employers and society, which also improves our earning ability. When I changed jobs after completing my PhD, I doubled my salary. Because I concentrated more on improving my skills and knowledge, I never worry about money now. I'm finally released from the trap of working for money, and it feels liberating. Working for money just to make ends meet makes us feel trapped.

We need to put ourselves in the position where we make money work for us. Unlike humans, money doesn't need to eat, sleep, and rest. It can work twenty-four hours a day and seven days a week on our behalf. That's why rich people always let money work for them.

In this book, I am going to pass along all the lessons taught by my money-smart brother and money-dumb brother — mistakes, wisdom, and knowledge. These lessons changed my life, and they changed the lives of my other brothers, sisters, and relatives too. Five of my brothers and sisters are becoming very wealthy. More than ten of my relatives are now millionaires. And because of them, I am on my way to achieving my financial independence.

Along with those lessons, I am sharing knowledge gained from my own investing experience and mistakes and my learning (a Bachelor of Arts in Accounting, a Master's in Finance, a Master's in Economics, a Master's in Computer Science, and a PhD in Business Administration). Finally, I blended those lessons with the knowledge and wisdom gained from reading more than 200 financial books.

This wisdom has changed my life and my family members' lives. It can change your life too. And you are probably wondering about those Chinese words on the cover. They mean "knowledge creates wealth."

Key Points in This Chapter

- You have everything you need to succeed.
- No one can stop you.
- You can achieve whatever you want.

知识创造财富

想

Chapter 1
You Become What You Think

*"Courage is the first of human qualities
because it is the quality that guarantees the others."*
Aristotle

When I was a child, my family had no money except a little income from selling eggs. We used it to buy necessities such as salt and soy sauce. Even though we had little money, we maintained a positive attitude toward life. We never let lack of money be an excuse for anything. Our mother's positive attitude was contagious among our family members. She taught us that we could produce everything we needed. It is not surprising that her positive attitude allowed her to give so generously to others. My money-smart brother followed her example in his own way and achieved great success. It took me awhile to learn to live by her example, but I was able to understand better as I experienced life's lessons.

If You Share, You Will Expand

My mother never let money issues or the lack of anything hold her back from doing what she thought was right. Even though we were poor, my mother was very generous and hospitable. When relatives or friends came to visit my family or do business in the local area, my family always welcomed them to stay with us. My mother would cook the best food for them. At that time, we never had a chance to

7

eat eggs ourselves because that was our merchandise to sell. But my mother served eggs to our friends, relatives, and even strangers.

When I grew older, I still could not understand the reasoning behind my mother's generosity. I questioned her about it. She said we should always treat friends with the best we could offer. Her generosity didn't stop with friends and family. My mother always donated money to charity. She believed in saving money and giving money to others. Even though she was not rich, she saved what she could over the years and donated lots of money to build roads and bridges.

She often said that we should not feel lack or limitations. We should share our best with others. If we gave what we could, we would have more. However, she did tell me that she always cooked the best food for our guests just in case they were not used to eating the plain food we normally ate at home.

My mother set a great example of helping others. She taught me that when you do good things for people, people will do the same for you. As a young boy, I helped a stranger push his cart to the top of the mountain. I knew how heavy his cart was. I used a cart to transport bamboo to town to sell. It takes more than one person to move a heavy cart to the top of a hill. I probably wouldn't have thought about helping him if my mother hadn't taught me to look for ways to help others.

As always, my money-smart and money-dumb brothers had different perspectives on our mother's generosity. My money-dumb brother never supported my mother's practice of treating others better than she treated us. When I was a child, I liked to go with him because he would eat at expensive restaurants. Of course, I really enjoyed the food he bought for the two of us. But the fact remained that my family needed food. We really should have shared our food with our whole family. I was too young at the time to realize this truth. Later on, I learned that if you share, you would expand.

My money-smart brother was different. He never felt he had any limitations. He always showed his love to my brothers and sisters, and he gave the best he could offer. His fascinating and inspirational success story itself proved that if you work hard, you can reach your dreams. He experienced difficulties and tough times like other poor children in China. But he had a big dream — a vision in his life. He altered his life by persistence and determination.

When my money-smart brother finished high school, he worked one year in our county's reservoir-building project. He went on to join the army after that. Later, he worked in a big city near Hong Kong and attended college there. He got a banking job after graduation. He worked very hard to advance from an entry-level job to a top management position in the organization.

His bank became the first bank in China to be listed in the stock market during 1980s. My brother saved most of his salary. He bought a lot of stock during that time, including his bank's stock. When the stock market went so crazy high in the 1980s, he automatically became a self-made millionaire. He was just twenty-seven years old.

My money-smart brother always gave us the best he could offer, even when he was poor. My most vivid memory of him demonstrating this value was the time he came home for a New Year's vacation when he was in the army. He bought gifts for every family member.

When my brother finished that first New Year's vacation at home, my mother and all of my brothers and sisters went to the train station to see him off. Because the train station was in a big city forty-five miles away, we needed to stay overnight in the city. He bought four hotel rooms for the entire family, just so we could say goodbye when he departed on the train. It sounded crazy at that time for a poor family to have four expensive hotel rooms. In fact, the hotel receptionist could not believe what she heard. She asked my brother to repeat the number of rooms we needed.

It was my first time to stay in hotel when I was a child. We felt like we were one of the richest families in our area. My mother was so excited. She repeated how proud she was of her son and how blessed she felt to have him. I decided then and there that I would work and study hard like my money-smart brother did. I wanted to give the best to my mother and my family too.

The Law of Attraction

What you believe shapes what you become. Your mind is the gatekeeper of your subconscious mind. What you think each day affects your actions. When you think positive, you will get positive results; when you think negative, you will get negative results. If you think you are rich, your subconscious mind will slowly change your way of thinking and acting to adopt ideas and practices that will lead you to become rich. I was so fortunate that my money-smart brother modeled how powerful and effective our thinking is. He never lamented over something he lacked. Instead, he always gave the best he could offer.

Life was not easy. There were so many problems when we were growing up in China. The economy was tough, it was not easy to find a good job, and it was hard to study at school. But most of the time, we created the problems in our own minds. I learned that the outside world is a reflection of our inner thoughts. We become exactly what we think about all the time. When people think they are not smart enough to study, they fail at school immediately. They become defeated in their own minds. When people think they do not deserve the best that life can offer, they are destined to be poor forever.

The Law of Attraction basically says like attracts like. Thoughts attract the same thoughts. People attract the same type of people they are. My money-smart brother's example of purchasing hotel rooms for his family on that first vacation home showed how the Law of Attraction works. By showing kindness, goodwill, and generosity, all of these good things will come back to you in the future. He always said we should try our best. He believed we should always send out blessings to others. He was convinced that when we do that, we would always receive the blessings from our work, school, friends, and family.

Even though I admired him, it took me a long time to learn to follow his advice. I fell into the trap of feeling entitled that someone owed me something instead of giving others my best. I had been stubborn from the time I was a child, so it took some time to change my thinking.

I was famous in my village for being stubborn and temperamental. When I was little, I did so many silly things. My family let me get away with it because I was the youngest. I was so spoiled. I still regret doing so many bad things. But people can change. I did, and the change was dramatic. Some people from my village remarked that I had changed into another man completely when I grew up.

I had an argument with my brother when I was seven years old. I was angry, and I wanted my mother to scold my brother. I thought of a way to get him in trouble. I went to my neighbors' house and hit their son on the head so hard, it made him bleed. I came back afterward and told my mother that my brother had just hit the neighbor boy on the head. But my plan didn't work.

That wasn't the only time I tried to get my brother in trouble. I intentionally hit my knee with a stone to make it bleed. I came back home and told my mother that my brother hurt my knee. I had second thoughts though. What if I had hit my knee and was seriously injured? What if I became handicapped just because I hit my knee? I grew concerned my mother would worry if I was seriously injured and bleeding badly. This didn't seem like such a good idea after all. I finally realized it was a bad idea to trick my mother into punishing my brother.

When I was ten, I went with my mother to my cousin's wedding. A boy was playing with a toy I wanted. When he didn't give it to me, I got mad. I stood outside my cousin's house for hours. It was winter, but I was stubborn and determined. I stood in the freezing wind and refused to go inside. My mother said, "Why are you so silly? It doesn't matter if the boy didn't give you that little toy. Why are you punishing yourself in the cold?" I stood my ground outside in the cold, but I didn't get the toy. I learned then that I can't have everything I want.

Another time, I started a fight with a neighbor boy. His father slapped my face. Shocked and scared, I ran to my mother. I was hoping she would make my brother beat up the boy's father. My brother refused. I felt like I was the victim. I cried and said, "If my father had not died so early, he would have beaten that man up for me." I felt insulted by the slap on my face.

My mother also felt insulted. She cried when my brother refused to beat up the man. I was devastated because I saw my mother crying. I didn't want to cause her sadness like that again. I never fought with anyone after that. I learned that once a fight starts, there will always be pain, injury, and sadness. I also learned I shouldn't mention things to my mother that would make her sad, such as problems, troubles, and failures. It taught me to take responsibility for my actions and come up with my own solutions to life's challenges.

I grew less temperamental as I got older, but I still had moments when my stubbornness got the best of me. My first job after high school showed me that I needed to change my thinking.

When I graduated from high school, I did not go to college immediately. Instead, I went to work in an entry-level engineering job at a company that was building the first factory in my county. Everyone applying for a job had to take an exam. We also had to deposit about $100 to the factory. My mother paid that money.

I got a very high score on the exam, so I was assigned the best job at the factory — directing the construction. My job initially was to copy the design of similar factories and then instruct people to build it. It was a very good job.

I worked diligently. I knew the opportunity for the job was priceless, so I showed my appreciation by unlimited dedication. I lived fifteen miles from the factory. I walked to work, so I had to get up very early to make it to work by 8:00 a.m. As a farm boy, I was accustomed to getting up at 5:00 a.m.

My nephew got sick one day, and I had to take him to the hospital on my way to work. He lived at the bottom of the mountain, and the hospital was close to the factory where I worked. It took three hours to transport him to the hospital using a one-wheel cart. After I took care of my nephew, I hurried to my office, but I was ten minutes late.

Unfortunately, my boss saw me. He asked why I was late. I was so young and naive at that time. No one told me that I should be careful about what I told him. Instead, I just decided to be myself and tell the truth. I reminded him that I was *only* ten minutes late. I told him I had a good excuse — I took my nephew to the hospital on the way to work. I explained that I got up at 5:00 that morning so I could still get to work on time.

He listened to my answer, but I knew he was not a patient man. Because of his position, he was regarded like a king. Everyone was afraid of him because he was our boss. He could decide our future: we could go to heaven (continue to work for him) or go to hell (go back home).

Instead of showing sympathy for my nephew and my difficult situation, my boss yelled at me for being late and daring to tell him I had an excuse. As punishment, he ordered me to go to work digging earth and building foundations for one month. When I heard his order, I was furious. I replied to him, "That's okay. I can do that digging job and actually, I used to work chopping bamboo. I am good at this kind of job!"

That month passed very quickly. I did an excellent job of digging dirt for the foundations and carrying it fifty yards away. Everyone in my group liked me, and we enjoyed the work. The job was really tough, but I did it. I survived because I remembered my money-smart brother telling me that I could be whatever I want. That gave me hope to continue, even though the conditions were hard.

Finally, I finished the last day of that month on the digging job. At 8:00 a.m. the next morning, I stormed into the director's office and told him, "One month has already passed. I did an excellent job over there digging earth. I'm ready return to my design job!"

He was furious that I would talk to him like that. No one had done that before. He lost his temper and yelled at me, "Get out and continue to do your digging job!" I lost my temper too and said, "You did not keep your word! I'm quitting this job and going home now!"

I left his office and went back home. I immediately regretted my decision. I realized I had made a big mistake, but I could go nowhere but home. I lost my precious job because of my bad temper. I felt I should have apologized to him, and then I wouldn't have lost my job. What should I do now?

When I went home, my mother did not say anything. I felt bad. She expected me to do well at this job, but I lost it. I stayed at home and helped my mother with her tasks, such as chopping bamboo poles, carrying them down the mountain, transporting them to the cities to sell, and buying food for my family.

Positive Thinking

After that event, I learned about the Law of Attraction. I realized I must change my thinking from negative to positive if I wanted to achieve success. I knew that losing my temper was the worst thing I could do. Anger could never solve any problems. Instead, an ill temper could exacerbate the situation. I paid a big price to learn the lesson about the Law of Attraction the hard way. Later on, I began to appreciate life more. I learned to show my gratitude to other people who helped me and cherish every opportunity I had.

That experience at my factory job changed me. I began to incorporate the lessons I learned into my life. I experienced positive changes as a result. I learned that my future depended on my own hard work and that no one owed me anything. I also realized that my success depended on how I responded to situations, even if I wasn't always treated fairly.

Even though we had not heard of the Law of Attraction at the time, the example that my mother and my money-smart brother set for me was powerful. They taught me to think positively regardless of the circumstances. And through their lessons on giving the very best of what they had, they taught me that I would ultimately attract good things into my life. I'm living proof that it works.

Key Points in This Chapter

- Think positively.
- If you share, you will expand.
- Dream big dreams.
- You deserve the best.
- You become what you think.

知识创造财富

独立

Chapter 2
Depend on Yourself

"That which we persist in doing becomes easier — not that the nature of the task has changed, but our ability to do so has increased."
Ralph Waldo Emerson

During the 2008 presidential campaign, Massachusetts' governor Mit Romney said that if you depend on someone, you were dead. It was a very important point. We forget this truth too often.

When I was a boy, my brothers and sisters worked hard to help my mother. We produced everything we needed and enjoyed our self-reliant life. We never depended on someone else — especially the government — to survive. My money-smart brother developed a fair system for us to work together. For example, we had to pick fresh grass to feed chickens after school. I had to pick ten pounds; one brother who is two years older than me had to pick twenty-five pounds; and another brother who is five years old than me had to pick fifty pounds. Before dinner, we would all work together to weigh everyone's collected grass. If we didn't collect our required amount of grass, we also had to face our punishment — we had to make it up the following day.

Working in the family business taught me a lot about depending on myself, but I didn't learn the pitfalls of depending on others until later. After I quit my job at the concrete manufacturing company, I traveled to Nanjing, Shanghai, to help my brother sell bamboo. What I learned completely changed my opinion about doing business.

My brother didn't know much about selling bamboo. One guy in our village told my brother that his relative needed a truckload of bamboo shoots. My brother ordered a large amount of bamboo shoots, and we set off to deliver them to Nanjing.

There were only three seats in the truck: one for the driver and the other two for my brother and the man who was helping us sell the bamboo. I had to lie on the bamboo shoots, under the cloth we used to cover the bamboo. The cloth kept the shoots from going bad. It would also hopefully prevent the bamboo from being stolen as well.

It took about twenty hours to drive from my hometown to Nanjing. I rode in the back with the bamboo all the way. The truck was hot, and the bamboo had a terrible stench. We arrived in Nanjing and stayed at a hotel for the night. When we were ready to leave the next day, the man who rode with us was nowhere to be found. All of our travel money — more than 2,000 Yuan — was gone.

To make matters worse, the bamboo shoots were going bad. Usually bamboo shoots last three days before they begin to spoil. We spent one day loading and one day driving to Nanjing. We had no choice but to sell the bamboo as soon as possible to the closest market. We left the truck at the hotel and took the bus to search for a buyer.

Around 5:00 p.m., I saw a man looking at me as if he knew exactly what I needed. He asked what I was looking for. I told him I needed a buyer for a truckload of bamboo shoots. He said he worked in the grocery store where I was going.

I gave him two packages of cigarettes to encourage him to ask his boss to buy the bamboo. Seeing the two packages of cigarettes, the man said he could still take me to see his boss, even if he had already gotten off work. I was hopeful.

By the time we got there, his boss was just about to leave for the day. I gave the boss two packages of cigarettes, hoping that he would consider buying the bamboo. The boss agreed to buy them. The boss wanted me to deliver the bamboo as soon as possible. He would wait at the store for the delivery.

I tried to take the bus back to my hotel. I was not familiar with the city and got lost. At almost 9:00 p.m., I found my way back to the hotel. By the time we delivered the bamboo shoots to the boss' office, he was angry and impatient. He said he didn't want to buy the bamboo because we took too long to deliver the shipment. I gave him two more packages of the best cigarettes to please him. Finally, he agreed to buy our bamboo at a very low price.

At the end of the transaction, we lost 30,000 Yuan in all. Initially, we didn't have enough money to buy the bamboo shoots we were reselling. My brother borrowed money from other people to pay for the bamboo. Now these people would be eager to get their money back. They didn't know we had lost so much money on our business deal.

When these people began to ask for their money, they looked first for my brother. When some of them couldn't find him, they began to threaten me. I hadn't worked in three months, so I didn't have any money. Even the driver said he would run me over with his truck because he didn't receive enough money to cover his trip to Nanjing.

You've probably guessed by now this was my money-dumb brother. I depended on my brother to make a good business decision and take responsibility for his actions. In the end, he didn't. It wasn't my fault, but I was guilty by association. This was my hard-earned lesson: never make a promise you are not able to keep. My mother said, "You should not have been helping your brother with his business. You should have gone to Shenzhen with your other brother." My other brother — my money-smart brother — was attending college in Shenzhen at that time.

Never Depend on Anyone

My money-dumb brother had a different opinion about self-dependence. He always said that we should depend on the government because it would provide all we needed. It could also give us the power to control other people. That might be true if someone worked for the government and became a politician. However, power or authority from the government was always abused by people. History has proven that in many countries where only a few people have all the power. It creates an environment where leaders become dictators.

In contrast, people in the United States have historically regarded holding a government job or serving as a politician to be lower-level positions. These roles were perceived to require fewer skills. Both Nona Webster and Benjamin Franklin wrote several articles talking about this issue. They supported the idea of a small government with limited power. They strongly stated that the United States should be governed by middle-class people. People who did not have money should not consider a career in politics.

When people in the United Kingdom went to vote a hundred years ago, candidates had to register how much property they owned and had to pay certain fees. People who were poor and could not pay the fees were not allowed to vote. Their leaders felt that people who could not earn enough money to support themselves or their families couldn't support the country or help it survive.

I learned another hard lesson about depending on others. I decided to go to Shenzhen with a friend to look for work. I kept asking him whether I needed any permits to go to Shenzhen. He said all I had to bring was my ID. I was only seventeen years old and naive, but he said he would take care of me.

When the day came, I left with 50 Yuan in my pocket. We boarded the train. We talked about many things on the trip. I loaned him some money to pay for his meal. It left me with only 20 Yuan. He promised he would pay me back as soon as we got there.

When we arrived in Guangzhou, he didn't even mention the money he borrowed. I had to spend 17 Yuan to buy my ticket from Guangzhou to Shenzhen. When it was check-in time, he boarded the train first. I got stopped because I did not have the required permit. It was clear now — I was conned.

My ticket expired because I did not get in the train on time, and I couldn't get a refund. It was getting dark. I had only 3 Yuan left in my pocket, and I had already run out of tears. After that, I resisted the urge to cry. I knew I had to be strong. I had to get back on my feet and come up with a plan.

I spent 2.86 Yuan in the post office to send a telegraph with a few words to one of my brothers: "I am in Guangzhou Train Station." Without any money left, I spent the night at the station. I awoke early the next morning. I was so hungry. I decided to make a deal with the woman who was selling bread in front of the train station:"I only have 0.14 Yuan, can you give me a piece of bread?" The woman looked at me. She gave me a piece of bread and said, "Go take it." I still gave her all the money I had.

Thousands of people crowded into the station that day. I was afraid my brother would not find me. Finally, I heard his voice over the train station intercom. I immediately felt safe. After meeting my brother, I gave the woman 5 Yuan for my appreciation (a piece of bread cost 2 to 3 Yuan at that time). I was so thankful for her kindness. I went to that station many times later on, but I never saw the woman again. That experience taught me that I should never depend on others. I also realized I should be more careful about the friends I choose.

Industry Pioneers Are Heroes

There are many professions from which to choose — doctors, teachers, nurses, and more. You can even start your own business and manufacture a product or provide a service. In the United States, common people consider people in industry to be heroes. If you asked children or college students whom they admire most, the answers would probably be Albert Einstein, Thomas Edison, or Bill Gates. With the exception of Abraham Lincoln, George Washington, or Thomas Jefferson, almost no one would choose politicians — even presidents such as George Bush or Bill Clinton. Most people believe that industry leaders or inventors create wealth, help history move forward, and contribute more value to society than politicians.

That opinion in third-world countries is different. Many poor people perceive that becoming a politician will provide them the influence that will make them wealthy. They find themselves lured by the power that an important political position offers. That attitude just lends itself to huge corruption problems.

When those people become politicians, they often expect more money from their government position. Unfortunately, the salary for politicians is not very good, so they are tempted to accept bribes. Unlike the United States, many countries do not have controls in place to monitor corruption. Many professions in the U.S. pay much better than politics; so people who are motivated strictly by wealth would not consider politics as their first career choice.

Wealth Is Not Created by Serving in Political Office

In third-world countries, politicians have greater power to do business and use the authority to help their friends or family create fortune. Unfortunately, other professions are not well-paid or not very well-developed. Because of this disparity, society inside these developing countries has created the false image that if you become a politician, you can become wealthy.

This is a very dangerous idea for society. Wealth is produced by common people who work hard performing real jobs to meet material needs in the countries' industries and service organizations — jobs that, in reality, are not created by politicians. People believe they can become powerful and get rich instantly by working for the government. There is no motivation to work hard when people can earn quick money simply because of their authoritative position. And a politician's ability to get rich quick in a corrupt environment is admired. It is unfortunate that honest, hardworking industry workers are less respected by society than people who work for the government. The real danger is that this mind-set can mislead a whole society to the point where a society could stop progressing. Everyone would just go to work for the government.

Historically, Americans have a healthier attitude regarding political leadership. Very few people consider that becoming a politician could lead to wealth. American politicians are regarded as servants of the people, and of course, it is not honorable to expect to get rich from this humble service.

Several former U.S. presidents went into politics after they became wealthy. For example, George Washington and Abraham Lincoln married very wealthy ladies and later became politicians. Herbert Hoover and Jimmy Carter became very wealthy due to their business success, and then they went on to become politicians. It's the same story with the Bush, Kennedy, and Roosevelt families.

Politics Is for Middle-Class People

When I was a child, my money-dumb brother always told me that I needed to work for the government to make my fortune. He showed me many examples in Chinese history and in our local communities where politicians became wealthy because of their positions. He always urged me to form connections with politicians. He believed we could use those relationships to do business and earn easy money.

I worked in a government job for more than five years where I supervised the financial industry in China. Family members, friends, relatives, and other acquaintances often asked me to do favors for their businesses or lend them money. It was kind of tempting, and it would be easy to get lost in the corruption. Several of my colleagues went to jail or had corruption problems because they misused their power as government employees.

I was so fortunate I resisted the temptations during that time. It was clear that if I continued to work in that position, I would constantly be approached to do unethical activities. I decided to quit that job. As expected, many people thought I was crazy to quit. But peoples' opinions did not matter to me at the time as I wanted to be myself

— and that meant being an honest person with integrity and strong character.

The Government Should Not be Hostile to Rich People

I find it interesting that the government is sometimes hostile to wealthy people. Some tax policies are designed to penalize rich people. In U.S. history, the government has sometimes tried to prosecute rich people. For example, during the first few years of Franklin D. Roosevelt's administration, the government filed lawsuits against wealthy people. Andrew Mellon (one of the wealthy targets) worked for three presidents as the Secretary of the Treasury Department. He was also the son of Thomas Mellon, the founder of Mellon Bank.

The case against Andrew Mellon was very famous. He was accused of avoiding tax. However, he made the tax law when he was in office. The investigation lasted more than five years, and it did not find any misdoings.

Andrew Mellon could afford to hire the best lawyers to represent him in court, so the government could not easily prosecute him. He finally told Franklin D. Roosevelt that he would donate his entire fortune if the government would stop the investigation. The case against Mellon tarnished the government's image, and it had a difficult time stopping all the wrongful prosecutions of the rich. But Franklin D. Roosevelt decided to accept Mellon's offer and ended the era of persecution and hostility toward rich people. The public was pleased that Roosevelt made the right decision to stop punishing wealthy people.

When the government thinks rich people are evil, no one is motivated to earn more money. My money-dumb brother was influenced by negative opinions about rich people. He often said, "Rich people are evil, so I do not like rich people." In reality, it is your right to be wealthy, and you deserve the best. As my money-smart brother said, "Money is not evil, but the love of money is evil. It is a shame to be poor."

Learn to Bless Rich People

In the beginning, I did not like Donald Trump because many people considered him to be a greedy hypocrite. Later on, I changed my negative attitude about rich people. I learned that when you like people, they will like you. If you hate people, they know it and will not like you either. This is another component of the Law of Attraction. Good people attract good people, and bad people attract bad people. If you do not like rich people, you will never become one of them. We should always look for the positive side of people and look past their negative aspects. By doing this, we will always find the goodness in any human being.

Life experiences have taught me that we should consider different opinions and bless people who are different from us. When we see a beautiful car, we should say, "Bless that beautiful car, bless that person who drives that car, and bless everything for that person." When we see a beautiful house, we should say, "Bless that beautiful house, bless the people who live in that house, and bless everything in that house." When we see a beautiful child, we should say, "Bless that beautiful kid, bless that kid's parents, and bless that kid's family." When we send out all blessings wherever we go, whatever we do, and to whomever we meet, we will receive blessings in return. The idea of giving blessings is also expressed in this phrase: "What you sow, you shall reap."

Market Entrepreneurs Changed the World

There were two kinds of business people in the United States during the nineteenth and early twentieth centuries: market entrepreneurs and political entrepreneurs. They always fought each other but finally, market entrepreneurs won public support. Political entrepreneurs sought and obtained wealth through the political power of the state. Their businesses were subsidized or granted monopoly status by the government. Of course, their production was not based on the real market's needs. Inevitably, their products and services were inferior and more expensive than the same goods or services from market entrepreneurs.

Market entrepreneurs, such as Cornelius Vanderbilt, John D. Rockefeller, Henry Ford, James Hill, Joseph Scranton, Charles Schwab, Andrew Carnegie, and Andrew Mellon, created big businesses that operated efficiently and produced low-cost, high-quality products and services. On the contrary, political entrepreneurs, such as Robert Fulton, Leland Stanford, and Henry Willard, used their political power to lobby in Washington. Their goal was to prevent real market competition while receiving subsidies and grants from the government.

The result? The market entrepreneurs changed the world and made history. They created wealth for common or poor people by developing business innovations that reduced costs. Henry Ford was one example. He produced automobiles. By using innovative production techniques, he reduced prices from $3,000 per car to just $500. His company produced more than 50 percent of the cars across the globe during his time. It is also important to note that many of the market entrepreneurs of Henry Ford's era donated most of their fortune to charities.

Key Points in This Chapter

- Never depend on anyone.
- Industry leaders are heroes.
- Wealth is not created by politicians.
- Politics is not easy for poor people.
- The government should not mistreat rich people.
- Learn to bless people.
- Market entrepreneurs changed the world.

知识创造财富

知识

Chapter 3
Knowledge is Power

"We need to learn to set our course by the stars,
not by the lights of every passing ship."
Omar Bradley

Both of my brothers emphasized education, but they had mismatched views about what people should learn. One focused on classroom and degree learning; the other emphasized skills training and knowledge application. Please remember that knowledge is power. You can learn whatever you want.

After I failed at my factory job, I went to Shenzhen to live with my money-smart brother in his apartment on campus. He was studying there at a university. Many young people in Shenzhen attended college at that time. Everyone there talked about their futures, new ideas, jobs, and studies. I envied the well-dressed students on campus.

I didn't have a plan for my life other than getting a job. I looked for a job my first week there but didn't find one. I felt discouraged and useless. After dinner one night, I told my brother I wanted to go back to study. I didn't expect my brother to take it seriously, but he did. To my surprise, he said he was willing to support me through school. I wasn't confident about my studying capabilities, but my brother believed in me. He said he would support me until I passed the college entrance exam and got admitted into college.

The first step was to take the entrance exam so I could go to college. That was an ambitious decision. No one in my village had ever passed the exam right after high school. Even my money-smart brother served in the army first and then worked in Shenzhen for two years before he decided to attend college. The entrance exam for his non-traditional bachelor's degree program was much easier. My brother supported my decision and offered to help. He knew how important college was to a successful future. He paid my tuition fee and sent me to school to study for the exam.

I hadn't been a great student in the past, and that was a big problem. When I was in high school and went to a big city for the first time, people laughed at me. I was from the country and didn't speak Mandarin well. At that moment, I realized I should study hard so I could be successful. Then, no one could ever laugh at me again. Like the old saying goes: "Those who laugh last, laugh the loudest." I didn't think laughter from other people should bother me. I decided to use the laughter to motivate myself. It encouraged me to study harder.

I thought I had some talent in math because I was the champion in a seventh-grade math contest. I still don't know how that happened. However, I didn't do well in math during my eighth-grade and ninth-grade years. My teacher always used me as an example. One time, she said, "Some people (me) came into school with a tremendous start — like a seventh-grade math champion — but now, they rank last in the class." That made me feel bad, but she was right.

Regardless, I was determined to take the high school entrance exam to see if I could make it. I scored one more point than the required score needed to advance. I didn't really want to go to high school, but my family insisted. I realized I needed to go to high school because I didn't want to work as a manual laborer at home.

Shaolin martial arts became popular when I was in high school. I became obsessed with it. I practiced martial arts in high school for two years. I spent lots of money buying martial arts magazines and books. During that time, I read more than 100 books and watched almost all the martial arts movies. I fabricated stories to convince my family to loan me the money that financed my obsession. I told them I needed money to buy some study books for class. I sometimes even felt bad because I lied to my family and didn't study hard at school. Needless to say, I wasn't a great student in high school. But things were different now. I was motivated to pursue a college education.

The first hurdle was preparing for the college entrance exam. I went to an exam preparation school in a nearby city. It helped students review materials and improve their exam scores. The entrance exam for college in China is notoriously tough. So many people want to go to college, but there are few colleges. Sometimes the acceptance rate was just 3 to 5 percent. That meant when one hundred students competed against each other, as few as three students could be admitted into college. Some of my brothers didn't go to school because they could not pass the test. They had to stay back in my hometown and work instead.

Studying for the entrance exam was terrifying. The competitive level of my classmates was fierce. Many people spent several years studying at the review school. One of my classmates spent eight years there studying for the exams. Moreover, most of them came from good high schools in big towns. I was from the worst high school in the rural area, where no one had ever been accepted to college right out of high school.

When I entered the review school, all the students took a test that assessed their knowledge level. There were fifty-five students in my class, and my test score ranked last. I told my money-smart brother that I wanted to quit studying. I felt it was impossible for me to pass the exam and get into the college. There were many students who studied two, three, and even eight years but still had not passed the exam. I did not want to waste his money.

He said I should just go. If I could not pass the first year, then I could continue to study the next year. I was afraid, but I was determined to study harder for my college entrance exams at that review school.

At the beginning, it was hard for me to follow along in class. My classmates were way ahead of me, and I knew nothing about subjects such as physics and chemistry. I concentrated on liberal arts subjects in high school but not on science. Finally, in the entrance exam, I chose liberal arts instead of science to avoid my weakness in science.

The review classes were fast paced, and we got tons of homework, exercises, and practices each day. The study environment was intense. All the students worked so hard. They knew they could go to college only if they could pass the entrance exams. For us, going to college was the equivalent of going to heaven. And if a student could not pass the exam, he had two choices. One choice was to return to his hometown to work for the rest of his life as a manual laborer. The other choice was to continue to study for the test at the review school. Continuing to study cost a large amount of money, but his future was still uncertain unless he could pass the test.

When the first semester was finished, we took the mock test again. Unfortunately, I was still the last person on the list. I wondered if I would ever catch up with my classmates, but I never gave up my hope of going to college. Actually, I did not mind taking mock tests even though I knew that I would be ranked last. My classmates had been at the school longer than me and spent an enormous amount of time preparing for this exam. But how could I catch up with them?

The thought of taking the tests haunted me every day even though I did not have time to consider whether I could pass. Maybe I did not want to think about the potentially disastrous result — I could fall in the majority of students who fail the exams. It was even more impossible for me — a simple farm boy — to pass this important test of intelligence and knowledge for college. But I still kept going, doing the homework, and going to classes because I still hoped that I might pass the exams. I decided to concentrate on today rather than worrying about tomorrow.

At that time, I didn't have the study skills to prepare for the exams. I was horrible at math, and I knew no English. And due to my low level of understanding — far below that of my classmates — I was not welcomed by most students. Even though I asked for help, very few students would share techniques with me for studying, preparing for the exams, and improving the test scores. Of course, they were busy with their own studies. Their pressure level was already enough for them; why should they care about others like me?

I did not have the money to buy additional review books for the exam. When I looked at the textbooks I had, I felt like daydreaming instead of learning. I knew I had to study hard, but it was still hard to pay attention. I decided the only solution to this problem was to copy the book. And that's what I started doing. I wrote down everything from the book in notebooks and took as many detailed notes as possible.

I had a desk I made from discarded bricks that I picked up from the farm fields. I sat down at my desk every morning after breakfast and started my task of copying the textbooks. Page by page, I read and rewrote each sentence. Next, I would read it back silently.

This method was boring and tough. The task seemed impossible because the textbooks were huge. There were seven textbooks for the five subjects we studied. It seemed like a small mountain. Most people would consider copying the textbooks by hand to be ridiculous or even stupid because the process was painstakingly slow. I could only copy five to ten pages each day, but this was the only way for me to study with the limited materials I owned.

In the beginning, it was hard to continue this arduous task. I copied a few lines and stopped. Then I continued writing a few more lines. I proceeded until my hands were almost bleeding and the pain became unbearable. I wanted to cry, but no tears came. I had to continue. I chose this method of studying for the entrance exams. It was the only way I could accomplish my dream of attending college. I had to fight for survival, and I had to pass the exams.

Every day, slowly but surely, I made some progress. I finished thirty pages in the first week and forty pages in the second week. Finally, by the end of the first month, I finished the first textbook. During the second month, I finished two more books. In total, I spent four months copying the content from all seven textbooks into my notebooks.

When the time came to take the mock exam again, my results were still very poor. I still ranked last in my class on the mock test. I was not sure whether my copying method I used for studying was working even though I invested four months in it. I still believed I made progress — judging by the huge number of notebook pages I used for copying the textbook information. I paid the price and worked hard, so I felt I deserved a positive outcome.

The program was ten months long and I had only six months until the formal entrance exam. If I continued using my study method of rewriting the textbook material, I projected that I needed four months to copy the material a second time.

I felt I had no other option. I had to work like a crazy man who did not know the outside world because he just wanted to ignore it and concentrate on his inner world.

I continued copying the textbooks into my notebooks and then reading the contents to myself. I finished copying all the textbooks a second time in just three months. That left only three months until the official exam. By the time we took another mock test, my score had improved. I ranked tenth from the last. I considered that to be great progress. At least I was not the worst student anymore.

The third time to copy all the textbooks into my notebooks took only two months. Afterward, I only had one month left until the official entrance exam. I stopped copying because I didn't have enough time to copy the textbooks one more time. I decided I would just review my copied notes.

After spending a few weeks reading through my notes, a miracle happened. When I read through my handwritten notebook pages, the contents of the textbooks were like printed pictures in my mind. When I finished reading the first line, I already knew the second line. When I finished the second line, I already knew what the third line said. It was like I had been sitting in a movie theater watching images of textbook pages during the last few weeks. The contents were repeated in my mind again and again when I read through them. I went through the notes repeatedly, and the review went faster each time. I must have read through the notes at least ten times. When I closed my eyes, the material was so clear that I could feel it, smell it, and even touch it.

Finally, it was the time for the real entrance exam. I had prepared for months, and it was worth it. I got very high scores. I passed the most important exam of my life. Eventually, I earned the ticket to college. Millions of Chinese people dream of such an opportunity. My score was way above the average score in my class of fifty-two students — I was ranked in the top 5 percent. The result was unbelievable, and it astounded my classmates. When my teachers and classmates asked me how I did it, I just showed them the small mountain of copied notebook papers. They were speechless.

There was one other factor in my success on the test. My roommate, Mr. Peng, studied with me. He was one of the people I knew who spent eight years studying for his college entrance exam. I didn't know what to do when I first started attending the classes. My math skills were really bad, but he helped me step by step to improve them. That is why I scored 85 — a pretty high score at that time. I don't think I would have done as well without his help.

Years later, I asked him why he helped me. He remembered the day he first arrived at the review school. He didn't have the 50 Yuan needed to attend school. The school was going to kick him out if he didn't come up with the money. I happened to have 50 Yuan in my pocket that my brother gave me. I loaned my roommate the money, even though we just met. I did not even know his name. He felt that helping me with my studies was the best way to repay the favor.

My journey to complete my entrance exam reminds me of a story I once heard. There was a young man who was ready to go to the outside world. The elder of the town gave him two notes. He told the young man to read the first note when he got to his destination and to read the other note when he came back. The young man did what the elder asked. Upon arrival, he opened the first note, which said "Don't be afraid." When he returned from his journey, he opened the second note. It said, "Don't feel regret." The moral of the story is that people should not feel regret when they have already made their choices. Once the opportunity is gone, it is gone forever.

We had a family rule: You had to go to college if you could pass the college entrance exam. There were only two options in my hometown for people to have a good life — to go college or to be a soldier. That is why I had the most unbelievable celebration after I passed the entrance exam and was admitted to college. That was probably the biggest event in my hometown at that time. That was my first time to achieve success through hard work and determination.

Key Points in This Chapter

- Always look forward.
- You don't achieve what you don't work for.
- Just focus on today.
- Concentration is the key.
- Repetition is the mother of learning.

知识创造财富

学习

Chapter 4
You Can Learn Whatever You Desire

"We all have possibilities we don't know about.
We can do things we don't even dream we can do."
Dale Carnegie

I passed the college entrance exams and entered college. It wasn't until then that I realized my money-smart brother was right when he said, "No one is smarter than you." My village people were wrong when they said that people from the village could not learn or pass the exam and enter college.

I worked at the department of finance for the state government after I finished my college degree. I held an accounting job the first year. My duty was to record all the expenses of provincial spending, which was subtracted from the tax income. At the end of the year, I had to report the result to the governor. I also had to prepare the budget for the following year.

There were no computers in our office at that time, so we used an abacus to do calculations. Because I dealt with a huge amount of numbers, I spent hours doing calculations and creating balance sheets. There were more than a hundred sheets of reports and budgeting information. A lot of the information was connected to information on other sheets. This made the job very tedious and challenging. Even the smallest mistake — a one cent difference, for instance — meant I had to spend three days and nights doing calculations to discover where the mistake was.

It was hard in the beginning. The endless calculations caused me headaches. Sometimes I was so tired and bored that I wanted to quit my job. I couldn't quit though. This job was a dream job that thousands of people wanted. After so many sleepless nights, I finally began to manage the demands of my job well.

Later, I realized the job gave me the best business training in the world. If you work hard, you can learn anything you want. My brother was right. No one is smarter or better than you.

Give No One Permission to Define Your Self-Worth

I made some major adjustments as a country boy entering the big city. I met people who frequently judged me based on my appearance or the way I spoke. Upon the first impression, they thought I might be ignorant because I was from the country. I was determined to give no one permission to devalue my self-worth — only I could define my self-worth. I never felt sorry for myself regardless of what others thought of me. Choosing to define my self-worth gave me more courage and determination to study and work harder. I wanted to become more successful than those people who looked down on me.

When I attended my first graduate school in 1993, publishing a book was almost impossible. I had an idea for a book about financial management in banks. I thought it could be a best seller. My classmates thought it was a crazy idea, but I never gave up hope. I went to the publishing company to discuss my book proposal. After several revisions of my proposal, they agreed to publish it. Even though it would be printed, we still had to market the book to sell it.

The most challenging thing was figuring out how to reduce the cost so we could make more profit. After talking with least five printing companies, we narrowed our choice to one company. I negotiated a very low price with that company, and they provided great flexibility in print quantity.

The next challenge was developing a marketing strategy so we could sell more books. We researched the addresses of all the banks in China — more than 5,000 in all. We created advertisements and mailed them to each of the banks. We also asked one of our fellow students to write an article about our book for one of the national newspapers.

We sold only few books at first. We thought we might fail. Slowly but surely, the number of orders increased. We eventually sold 8,000 copies. Back then, selling that many books was a miracle. Selling so many books reinforced our belief in ourselves and the value of our book.

You Deserve the Best Things This World Can Offer

It is your birthright to have everything the world can offer. You deserve the best, so don't sell yourself short.

Graduate school was challenging. I got up at 6:00 a.m. each morning, went running, and then read English. I scheduled most of my courses in the afternoon. My evenings were spent reviewing lessons and doing homework.

I worked at a state government agency after my graduate study in China. During that time, I often asked myself, "Is this the life I wanted?" My conscious mind said, "Yes. The job paid well. It was stable and provided a good retirement plan." However, my inner voice — my subconscious mind — said, "No. The job was not interesting or challenging, and I did not feel fulfilled. I had a powerful position that people dreamed to have, but I was bored and it did not interest me."

I had dreamed of studying overseas for many years. My desire grew after I completed my first master's degree in China. My graduate study experience made me more knowledgeable about what to expect. It also increased my confidence about my abilities. I was more realistic, intelligent, and steady. It prompted me to re-evaluate my life and caused me to cherish it more.

Many people live their lives with no hope. They either lack opportunities or they do not have the courage to take advantage of opportunities. I felt blessed. I was able to earn a good education in China, but I felt called to do something greater.

I was drawn to the United States by hopes of new opportunities. I knew I could alter my life if I worked hard. Even though my future was not certain, I could control my life with my own abilities. I chose this path for myself, so the only one that I could blame was myself if I failed. And I knew that if I failed, it would be because I did not work hard enough to seize the opportunity.

So I made a second life-changing decision — to quit my job and come to the United States to study. My colleagues and my brothers and sisters thought I was crazy for several reasons: I was just promoted to a supervisor position, I was already thirty years old, and I did not know how to speak much English.

Moving to America was a big life decision. I would start from nothing again. This was not a foreign concept to me since I grew up in a poor family. Nevertheless, I knew I would never regret my decision to quit my good Chinese government job and study in the United States.

So I came to the U.S. in 1998 and continued to explore this new world. As a result, I found fulfillment. That decision challenged me and made my life more interesting. It felt wonderful to have a chance to start a new life.

It was exciting, but it was tough too. I tried to avoid working off campus during school because it took too much time away from my studies. I worked over the summer instead to earn money to pay for school. One summer, I worked at a restaurant in Maryland. I was so tired every day after I got off work. I couldn't even walk. All the workers shared the tips and the other two servers were lazy. I didn't like the idea of sharing my tips with servers who didn't work hard.

Later on, I found a different job at a new restaurant in Detroit. This job was better because I got to keep all the tips I earned. It was still hard work because I had to please my customers to earn better tips.

To make things tougher, I developed a terrible blister from sitting on a long Greyhound bus trip from Maryland to Detroit. I ended up needing minor surgery because of it. To save some money after my operation, I chose to walk for two hours from the hospital instead of taking a taxi. My boss gave me two bags of rice while I was recovering from my surgery, but I had to get up and cook my own meals.

Even though I was hopeful and inspired by the opportunities, the first semester at graduate school in the United States was terrible. I was totally lost in my classes and did not understand what the teacher was saying. Sometimes, I did not even know what the homework was. Every day brought new challenges because I lacked good English skills. I struggled to take notes in class, do homework, and take tests. There were emotional challenges too. I had no one to talk to and no one to help me solve any of my problems. I had to rely on a very strong will to continue daily tasks and overcome all these challenges.

It was a great challenge to survive graduate school. I always had too much to do and too little time, so I had to study every day without a break. There was no ending and no beginning.

I was able to struggle through because I knew millions of people wanted to study, but they did not have a chance. I now had this great opportunity to change my life and achieve something bigger than myself. I had to do my best. I appreciated the opportunity very much and worked twice or three times as hard as other people did. The challenges did not matter to me though because I felt so blessed. If I failed, I could blame no one but myself.

No One Can Stop You. Only You Can Stop Yourself!

After finishing my second master's degree in Economics, I changed my major to Computer Science. I believed the knowledge of computers could help me in the future. Computer Science was difficult for me because I did not have any background in the subject. I didn't even know how to use Microsoft Word when I started graduate school. But when I decide to do something, I just go forward, even if I face difficulties.

The first semester in Computer Science was all right. However, one class I took in the second semester was extremely difficult. If I failed this required class, I would have to quit the program.

The instructor gave us fifty questions the week before the first test. The test the next week included thirty out of the fifty questions. There was one catch: we had to answer the questions exactly the same as the answers he had provided the week before. I was thirty-five years old and had never faced a situation like this before. I tried my best. Unfortunately, the answers were too long, and trying to answer so many questions was confusing. I only answered sixteen out of the thirty questions, which meant I failed the test. It was very frustrating. If I failed the second test, I would probably fail the class.

The second test was approaching. I was scared to death, but I had to face it. I felt frustrated that I could not memorize the answers to fifty questions. I was still trying to learn English, which didn't make things any easier. I tried and tried, but I was still unable to manage these fifty questions. I even cried several times. It seemed impossible to pass this class, but I had to fight for my grade. This battle would determine my future. If I failed, I had to quit the program. The worry overwhelmed me.

Around 2:00 in the afternoon — just twenty-four hours before the test — I decided to start working no matter what the outcome might be. Once I started studying, I forgot about everything else. I just concentrated on the test. I sat at my desk with the fifty questions and answers. They were on five sheets of paper, and each sheet had about ten questions. I spent five minutes on each question and tried my best to memorize the answer before moving on to the next question. I read each question more than five times, word by word. It took more than five hours to go through all fifty questions.

I took a break and went home for dinner. By the time I finished the meal, it was almost 8:00 p.m. — just eighteen hours before the test. I settled back in and spent another five hours studying.

When 1:00 a.m. arrived, I was very tired and could not keep my eyes open. I was still not sure I could manage these fifty test questions. I could not go to sleep until I memorized them. If I did, I would fail the test.

I drank a cup of coffee and tried to stay awake. Half asleep, I struggled to memorize these fifty questions, one by one. It was tough, but I had to survive this test. By now, I was working through all fifty questions for the third time. I finished around 8:00 a.m., but I was still unsure about each question. After eating breakfast, I felt I had to continue working since I only had six hours left until the test.

This time, I changed my strategy. I just reviewed the fifty questions without looking at the answers. When I read the question, I tried my best to find any clues to help me answer the questions. I tried for five minutes to answer the first question, but I couldn't. Then I reviewed the answer I had put aside.

I thought of another tactic: I decided to use fewer than ten words to summarize the answer. I figured that if I looked at these words that were part of the full answer, I could answer the related question completely. Even if I could only recall these ten words, when the instructor saw these words, he would hopefully realize I knew something and would at least give me partial credit.

It took almost four hours to generate ten words to memorize for each question. I now only had two hours left before the test. I was not hungry or thirsty, but my mind was very clear. I felt a sense of urgency to memorize fifty questions and survive this test. I was still not sure of each question, but I had to try my best, no matter what.

This time, I read the first question without looking at the answer. Then I closed my eyes and visualized the answer. Next, I tried to visualize the ten words I wrote for each question. I searched in my mind to find these ten words and expand them into the full answer.

This had to move quickly. If I looked at the question and could not remember the answer, I marked that question wrong. If I knew the answer for that question, I would move to the next question.

It took almost an hour to finish this step. I marked the twenty-five questions I could not answer. Now with only one hour left, I had to focus on these twenty-five questions.

I was completely alert. I knew I could succeed if I continued the way I was working. I already made huge progress by memorizing half of them.

Finally, I succeeded in memorizing all fifty questions just before the test. I went to class and sat down to take the test. I read the first question, closed my eyes, found the answer in my mind, and then wrote down the answer precisely. I read the next question, closed my eyes again, found the answer in my mind again, and wrote it down. I followed the same process for all thirty questions.

I was the first person to finish the test. The following week, I found out that I was the only person who scored a perfect 100. The teacher thought that was unbelievable because the answers were exactly the same as the original answers.

I used the same method to prepare for the next text. The instructor told us that we could bring only our pens or pencils to write the answers. He did not believe I could have gotten that grade. But again, I got 100 on the next test.

I finished this class with an A+ because I scored 100s on all three tests. The instructor was astounded by my ability to take his tests. He said I was the only person who could answer his questions without any mistakes during his thirty years of teaching.

Key Points in This Chapter

- Define your own self-worth.
- You deserve the best this world can offer.
- Wake up the achiever inside you.
- Never, never, never give up!
- You are the captain of your own destiny.

知识创造财富

钱

Chapter 5
Managing Money Is a Skill

"If you think education is expensive, try ignorance."
Derek Bok

My money-smart brother told me that handling money is the first skill anyone should learn. When I was a child, my family was very poor. I always wanted to change my life because I didn't want to be poor forever. Becoming financially independent seemed like a dream that would never come true for a farm boy.

Based on my money-smart brother's advice, I sought financial independence. That's why I worked harder. I made a good salary when I worked for the government, but I never thought of saving money. It was my opinion back then that becoming wealthy depended on luck when gambling or buying stocks — not saving and investing.

Actually, I never thought that learning to build wealth was a necessary skill for common people like me. China's stock market started booming in the 1980s, and some people became rich overnight. I waited for stock market booms to make me wealthy but, of course, it never happened. And I did not save any money when I worked for the government. I didn't think that earning a modest interest rate on savings was enough to make anyone financially independent.

Everyone around me had this mediocre mind-set, which further influenced me. They earned, spent, and left nothing. Some people saved money, but it was not enough to catch up with the inflation. Other people around me did not like the idea of being wealthy. They thought money was evil and rich people were greedy. I never liked this idea very much because I knew some rich people who were very nice. Nevertheless, it influenced my subconscious mind. I gradually began to believe that I too might dislike some rich people.

The biggest dream I thought I could achieve was finishing my education, finding a job, and earning a salary. I never thought my life could be something bigger. Deep in my heart, I had already given up on the dream of becoming wealthy. I still wanted to be financially independent later on, but I believed it was a faraway dream. I wasn't sure it would ever be a reality for me.

I spent eight years working on my graduate studies when I came to the United States, so I was very broke. When I was practicing my English one day, my roommate suggested I try a different method of improving my language skills. He suggested I find some materials that I could listen to and also read. I thought that sounded like a good idea, so I asked him if he had anything I could try.

He had some materials, but he thought I might not like them. I told him I wanted to try them anyway. He turned on his computer and showed me what he had. Then he asked me what subjects I liked most. I told him that I would probably prefer business or money topics. He copied the files for the materials on my flash drive. I put it in my bag and forgot about it.

I was very busy with school at that time. I always had too much studying to do during my tough PhD program. One night about four weeks later, I did not have much to do. It occurred to me that I should check out the materials my roommate gave me.

One of the audio books I listened to was *Think and Grow Rich* by Napoleon Hill. I had never heard this kind of information. I was shocked by the idea that common people could become wealthy. I was so excited that I finished the whole audio book. Then I continued to listen to the second audio book — it was *Rich Dad, Poor Dad*. Again, I was shocked by the idea of becoming rich. After I finished listening to both of them, I found both hard-copy books and started reading them immediately. It took me two days and nights to read them.

This marked a turning point in my life. These two authors said anyone could become wealthy. It did not matter what we are doing right now, how poor we are, where we are from, or how well-educated we are. What mattered was our thinking. Both books said that being wealthy is our birthright, and it is a shame to be poor.

Reading these two books changed my life. I realized I wasted forty years of my life because I was so ignorant. Getting wealthy requires knowledge and skill, and everyone can learn and master it.

Those two books entered my life at the perfect time because I had a new job and faced some decisions about handling money. If I had read books like these when I worked for the government, I would not have been so poor then. I now understood I had to manage my own money and control my future. I would never again make the same mistakes I made in my first forty years.

Before reading those books, I almost bought a new car. After reading those books, I was grateful I didn't. As I continued to read personal finance books and educate myself about money, I realized buying a new car was a bad decision. I learned that when you drive a new car off the dealership parking lot, it depreciates 20 percent.

One morning when I was jogging, the church pastor introduced me to a well-to-do lady and her two kids. When the pastor left, we continued jogging. We discussed the money issue, and I told her I was thinking of buying a new car. She told me that her family would never buy new cars. They always bought cars that were one or two years old because they cost so much less. As a matter of fact, she had just bought a two-year-old car for her family.

She also shared how they invest their money. She and her husband only bought mutual funds. She suggested that Vanguard was worth considering. When we finished jogging, she recommended I check out Dave Ramsey's personal finance books. She thought I might find them easy to understand.

I read Dave Ramsey's book, *Total Money Makeover*, several weeks later. It taught me how to choose retirement and educational funds, save money, and gain financial independence.

All three of these books changed my life forever. I knew I would never be poor again. I learned it was shameful to be broke and borrow unnecessary money. I realized I could one day achieve my financial dream through knowledge and understanding. I would never again live without hopes and goals.

Key Points in This Chapter

- Managing money is a skill anyone can learn.
- Money is not evil.
- You will grow when you try something new.
- Mistakes give us our greatest learning opportunities, but we must avoid repeating them.
- Financial independence is a choice.

知识创造财富

知识

Chapter 6
Financial Knowledge

"Take action. Seize the moment. Man was never intended to be an oyster."
Theodore Roosevelt

My money-smart brother taught me that we should always find ways to learn and improve our financial knowledge. During a visit one day to my Toastmasters club, a gentleman gave away a few tickets for a business seminar at the Jackson Convention Center. I was lucky that day and won a ticket. I was excited — the seminar featured a former Microsoft executive, former New York City mayor Rudy Giuliani, and renowned business speaker Zig Ziglar.

It was hard to wait until the day of the seminar. Unfortunately, I had to teach two classes that day, but that was manageable. I got up at 6:00 a.m., skipped my morning jog, and arrived at the convention center at 7:00 a.m. There were thousands of people already waiting. I traded in my ticket at the counter for an entrance pass and joined the throng, talking with other people excited about the event. Then, I went back to my university to teach my 8:00 class.

I returned to the seminar after I finished teaching my morning class. I missed two speakers while I was gone, but I was able to hear every other speaker on the schedule until the lunch break. I left one more time to teach my 2:00 class. As much as I wanted to hear the famous speakers on the schedule for early afternoon, I decided I simply couldn't cancel my classes. It has always been important to me to fulfill my teaching responsibility.

When I got back to the seminar, I was disappointed to learn Zig Ziglar had already finished speaking. But I told myself, "Move on. Keep going. Never let the negative thinking stop you." Suddenly, my attitude changed from negative to positive, and I enthusiastically listened to the rest of the seminar.

Luckily, the final few speakers were great. Rudy Giuliani was among them. I was especially impressed by one speaker, Phil Town. He spoke about achieving financial freedom, a major interest of mine. Town talked about how he went from working at a job with a $4,000 annual salary to becoming a millionaire in five years. He did that by learning how to invest, courtesy of a wealthy man he met at his job. His story was fascinating — almost a miracle. After his talk, he invited listeners to sign up for a two-day investment workshop for $100. Hundreds signed up, and I was among them. I would never miss any opportunity to learn.

The workshop took place all day Saturday and Sunday that same week. More than 500 people assembled amid a buzzing excitement. Phil Town did not teach that workshop. This one featured different speakers. I started to have mixed feelings about what the speakers were teaching since I already knew the topic of investing fairly well. I strongly believed in long-term investing, dollar cost averaging, long-term economic improvement, and investing in mutual funds. These speakers instead talked about options trading, market speculating, and short-term buying and selling.

Since I paid $100 and believed there was still something worthwhile to learn, I cleared my mind and listened like someone who is totally new to these topics. I learned a lot and came to understand several things I had not fully grasped before. I made a number of friends who are business owners and entrepreneurs. I loved being around these types of people. I still keep in touch with some of them.

After the two-day workshop, the speakers offered attendees the opportunity to sign up for the next levels of options investing training: a Master's level at $5,000 tuition and a PhD level at $30,000. More than twenty people signed up for higher-level training sessions since the workshop was so exciting and entertaining. I didn't have that kind of money. Instead, I went to a nearby bookstore after the workshop and bought one of the best options trading books, *Options Made Easy*.

I was not entirely convinced by what the workshop speakers said. I went to Mexico to renew my U.S. visa the following week. I read the options book on my bus trip and thought about investing almost every minute of my journey. After all my years of study, I couldn't believe this two-day options trading workshop could easily destroy my investing belief system.

Admittedly, there was something wrong with my investing system, and that's why options trading could distract me. Having discovered this, I suddenly had a burning desire to seek out the perfect method of investing. I realized this knowledge was important to everyone, including me. If mutual fund and dollar cost average investing didn't work, all my retirement savings, educational funds, and other investments would be gone.

I endured a sleepless twenty-hour bus trip back from Mexico. I arrived at 4:00 a.m., grabbed a few hours of sleep, and went to the bookstore around 11:00 a.m. I strongly believe if you want to reach the top in any field, you need to know what the top ten people in that field are doing. I already knew the top investors were Peter Lynch and Warren Buffett.

I should confess my understanding of Peter Lynch. He wrote two books: *One Up on Wall Street* and *Beating the Street*. Both are good, but reading the first book is always strongly recommended. I did not know this at the time. I only bought his second book, *Beating the Street*. It was a mistake to read that book alone.

I decided to read Peter Lynch's *One Up on Wall Street*. I finished the book in one sitting at the bookstore. After more than ten hours of reading, I came back the following day to read *The Warren Buffett Way: Investment Strategies of the World's Greatest Investor*. It is also strongly recommended by most investment people. It was also a good book and reinforced the basics of value investing — the same focus of Peter Lynch's book.

After two days of reading, I was frustrated. I was almost ready to surrender to this new strategy of options investing I learned in the workshop, even though Peter Lynch and Warren Buffett disagreed with the practice.

The next day, I went back to the bookstore. This time, I attacked a book I had noticed the day before, entitled *Breaking the Jewish Code*. It was about how to live well and achieve happiness in life.

I noticed another book nearby, *Rule #1* by Phil Town. I am always curious about books, so I picked it up too. I bought a cup of tea and started reading. I thought I'd take just five minutes to skim *Rule #1*, but found I couldn't stop reading. I didn't want to skip even a word. Town's book was totally different from his workshop. I gladly bought the book on the spot even though I'm typically a frugal guy who much prefers buying discounted books on eBay. I was convinced it would prove important to my investing.

After reading Phil Town's *Rule # 1*, I had a much more complete understanding of investing, including matters of value investing and dollar cost averaging. For the vast majority of people, options and futures should be considered to be speculating, not investing.

You probably realize by now that I have a passion for learning. Because of this passion, I spent a week attending business seminars and a week reading four important investment books. You may think the way I went about these tasks was strange. You may think it is unnecessary to comment in so much detail. Most people would not spend whole days reading at the bookstore when they have little money to buy books. But the story is here because it speaks simply and clearly about one vital theme: passion.

Abraham Lincoln once said, "Happiness is a choice. You can choose to be happy, or you can choose to not be happy." So please choose positive thinking. Act as if you will never fail. Find something you love to do, and live with passion.

Key Points in This Chapter

- Keep going.
- Find out what's really going on.
- Never give up.
- Be thirsty for knowledge.

知识创造财富

健康

Chapter 7

Be Healthy

*"One of the secrets of life is to make stepping stones
out of stumbling blocks."*
Jack Penn

My money-smart brother told me that in order to enjoy your wealth, you need to take care of your health. In your life, you should achieve physical health, financial freedom, and spiritual peace.

Every Health Problem Starts from Within

When I finished college in China, I was fortunate to get a job working for the Chinese government. I was satisfied with my job, and it paid me well. The only negative aspect of the job was that I was expected to drink and smoke with the clients. I was only twenty-five years old at that time. I worked hard every day. I was never concerned about my own health. To tell the truth, I didn't even know what the word "health" meant. Consequently, I did not pay much attention to it. But my carelessness did not last for long.

One day, I experienced a stomach pain so severe, I had to visit the doctor. After my checkup, the doctor said, "We need to perform some blood tests." One week later, I learned I had a serious problem with my stomach and might need surgery. I was shocked to hear this news because it was unexpected and I had not been sick before. I was feeling fine before my stomach pain. I thought I was healthy.

My health problem reminded me of my hometown, a small village in the mountains of eastern China. People in this town lived healthy lives. They produced everything without using any chemical pesticides. Most of the time, people ate vegetables and wild fruits. They also raised pets and animals such as chickens, ducks, and lambs in their backyard.

People in this town walked more than five miles each day to work in the mountains. Even today, I remember walking with my mother to the top of the mountains to pick fresh tea tree leaves. We had to get up very early in the morning, and the leaves were still wet with mountain dew when we picked them. After we gathered them, my mother baked the leaves immediately. I always helped her ignite the fire by feeding the wood stove.

It is intriguing that the word "disease" was nowhere in their dictionary. I believe this is because people in my village never thought about getting sick. People were healthy because they ate fresh food, drank natural green tea, and performed manual labor in the mountains every day.

Since people in this village rarely got sick, their life expectancy was higher than other places. The average life expectancy of the older generation there was more than eighty-five years old. My grandfather lived to the age of eighty-nine, and my uncle died at the age of ninety-three. One of my aunts is now eighty-eight years old. Even our neighbors lived to be ninety years old. Two neighbors are now eighty-five and maintain healthy lives.

Everything Happens for a Reason

But what happened to my generation? Four of my brothers are overweight, and two have diabetes. One of my brothers has lung cancer. And I had a serious stomach problem by the time I was twenty-five years old.

Because of these health issues going on within my family, I started analyzing them. I learned the reasons behind what was happening to my brothers and me. First, we lived in cities and did little physical activity. We never made the extra effort to walk places. We traveled everywhere by car. When we had to go upstairs, we took an elevator.

We also smoked tobacco and drank alcohol every day. To make matters worse, we ate out almost every day and never cooked at home. Restaurants meals were larger portions than we would have fixed at home, so it caused us to consume too much food. When I was a child, we ate three meals at the same time every day. We stopped eating immediately when we felt full. We never ate too much.

We are responsible for our own actions, and we often create our own health problems. After realizing this, I made a life-changing decision: I would take control of my health, so I would never need to see the doctor again. I took action immediately. I quit smoking and drinking, ate healthier food, incorporated physical activity into my daily routine, and maintained a positive attitude about life. After a month, I went back to the doctor for a checkup. He said I was in perfect health. I have not had to visit the hospital for more than fifteen years now. I feel young, healthy, and energetic every day. This chapter contains the basic rules I follow.

Exercise Thirty Minutes Each Day

Jogging alone can reduce many health problems, including being overweight, diabetes, and heart disease. I used to jog outside, but the weather wasn't always right for it. I bought a treadmill, so now I can jog anytime. You might not enjoy jogging, so try other types of exercise until you find something that motivates you to move.

It takes a lot of knowledge to maintain a healthy lifestyle. I went to a Tony Robbins seminar in Chicago last year and learned a lot about being physically fit and healthy. After that, I bought four recommended books to start educating myself more on health issues: *Who Gets Sick; Eat, Drink, and Be Healthy; The Answer to Cancer;* and *If You Could Hear What I See.* After reading these books, I now understand that most diseases are caused by overeating, eating unhealthy food, smoking, and lack of physical activity.

In the book, *If You Could Hear What I See: Lessons about Life, Luck, and Choices We Make*, the story of the author's struggle with her illness is fascinating. The author, Kathy Buckley, survived a terrible car accident. Then, she developed cancer. She went through the first treatment session, but she could not stand the painful process anymore. She quit going to the treatments and dealt with the disease herself.

She focused on eating properly and maintaining a positive attitude, but most importantly, she took an aerobics class. As she finished the class, she began to see the positive consequences of exercising. She fell in love with the idea of being healthy by increasing physical activity. Interestingly, she started teaching that aerobics class. When she went back to the hospital for a checkup one year later, she learned she was cancer-free.

Eat a Diet That is Seventy-Five Percent Fresh Fruits and Vegetables

I learned how to cook and read books on how to prepare healthy meals. I learned that seventy-five percent of my food intake should be fresh fruits and vegetables. There is a program called "5 a Day for Better Health" that was developed in the United States to encourage people to each more fruits and vegetables. Walter C. Willett, MD commented on this program in his book, *Eat, Drink, and Be Healthy*:

> Back in 1991, the National Cancer Institute launched its 5-a-Day public health campaign. Through grocery store banners, labels on fruits and vegetables, public service announcements in the media, and educational materials for school children, it urges us to eat five servings of fruits and vegetables a day. This campaign, which is still going strong, has been incorporated into the USDA Food Guide Pyramid, as well as into guidelines from the American Heart Association, American Cancer Society, World Health Organization, and others.

Five a day is a good start. But it gives no real guidance on what qualifies for five a day. Two glasses of orange juice, an apple, an order of French fries at lunch, and a potato with dinner meets the 5-a-Day target. But while it's better than no fruits and vegetables at all, it doesn't offer the full dose of health benefits described here.

Dr. Willett suggested that we use five servings a day as a minimum, not a goal. Don't include potatoes, sweet potatoes, and French fries in your daily tally because they include too much sugar. He also suggested varying the fruits and vegetables in our diets.

Drink Only Green Tea and Water

Green tea and water are still considered the top two healthy drinks after thousands of years because they are sugar-free. Here is what *Eat, Drink, and Be Healthy* says about green tea:

> According to Chinese mythology, Emperor Shen Nung discovered how to make tea in 2737 BC, using the leaves of the plant known today as Camellia sinensis. Nearly five thousand years later, tea ranks second as the most-drank beverage in the world, right behind water. The health-promoting properties long ascribed to tea are only now receiving the careful scientific scrutiny they deserve.

> Some of the benefits in tea include a gentle mental and physical pick-me-up and lower risk of kidney stones and gallstones. Some studies have suggested that drinking green tea may lower rates of some cancers, particularly stomach cancer.

A Secret of Living a Long Life

I read an article that suggested one-third of Americans today are overweight and have diabetes. It noted these two conditions are responsible for $150 billion in medical costs each year. Ten years from now, the medical costs for diabetes will be double what they are today. That's why First Lady Michelle Obama started a program called "Let's Move." Major diseases, such as heart disease, cancer, and diabetes, are preventable in most cases. People can reduce their risk of developing these diseases simply by taking positive actions. Eating properly, avoiding cigarettes and alcohol, and exercising can reduce the chances of developing these diseases. Physical fitness is one of the basics for success in every area in life.

I want to conclude this chapter with a story from *John D: A Portrait in Oils and Success through a Positive Mental Attitude*. John D. Rockefeller, once the richest man in the world, was diagnosed with stomach problems when he was fifty-five. His doctor said he would only live for twelve months. He decided to retire from his business entirely, and he developed a system to stay healthy.

- He attended Baptist church services every Sunday and took notes to learn the principles that he might apply daily.
- He slept eight hours every night and took short naps every day. The rest helped him avoid harmful fatigue.
- He took a bath or shower every day. He was neat and clean in his appearance.
- He moved to Florida, a climate conducive to good health and longevity.
- He lived a well-balanced life. He absorbed fresh air and sunshine while he engaged daily in his favorite outdoor sport — golf — and indoor activities, such as games and reading.
- He ate slowly and in moderation. He chewed everything well. It allowed the saliva in his mouth to mix with the foods and liquids. It also ensured they were well-digested and swallowed at body temperature. He avoided foods that were too hot or too cold for the mouth to protect his stomach.
- He digested mental and spiritual materials. He said blessings at each meal. And at dinner, he asked his secretary, a guest, or a member of his family to read the Bible, a sermon, an inspirational poem, or a motivating passage from a newspaper, magazine, or book.
- He employed Dr. Hamilton Fisk Biggar full time. Dr. Biggar was

paid to keep John D. well, happy, and alive. The doctor motivated his patient to develop a cheerful, happy attitude.

- He didn't want the members of his family to inherit the hatred of his fellow man. Therefore, he began sharing part of his possessions with the needy. At first, Rockefeller's motive was primarily a selfish one — he wanted a good reputation. Then something happened! By acting generously, he became generous. And by bringing happiness and health to many through his charitable and philanthropic contributions, he found happiness for himself. The foundations he established will benefit mankind for generations to come. His life and money were instruments for good. This world is a better place for people to live because of him.

Through this meticulous system, John D. Rockefeller maintained his health and happiness. Surprisingly, he lived to be ninety-seven years old — forty-two years past his diagnosis!

Key Points in This Chapter

- Our level of health is directly connected to our lifestyle and eating habits.
- Everything happens for a reason.
- Exercise at least thirty minutes each day.
- Seventy-five percent of your food intake should be fresh fruits and vegetables.
- Green tea and water are the healthiest beverages we can drink.

知识创造财富

事实

Chapter 8
Ten Fallacies about Money

*"If we all did the things we are capable of doing,
we would literally astound ourselves."*
Thomas Edison

I was broke for so many years. I decided to learn to become financially independent, but I was far from achieving that goal. Even after I completed my PhD and changed my job, I still had a long way to go. I knew I could get there because my money-smart brother had achieved financial independence. Thousands of people had proved it was possible and accomplished their financial goals.

Getting there still puzzled me. It was clear for years that one of my brothers was money-smart and the other was money-dumb. When I was a child, they influenced me a lot. I often asked them for advice.

I rarely returned to China after I came to the United States to go to school. The first time, I did not return to China for more than ten years. Everything there was different from what I remembered. Our brothers and sisters did not get together very often after our mother died. So when I decided to visit, my brothers and sisters got so excited. They all met me at the airport.

After several minutes of catching up, we needed to decide where I should stay. I had two choices since both my money-smart brother and money-dumb brother lived in the city. My money-dumb brother quickly told everyone that I should stay in his home, and I agreed. It did not matter to me since my mother was gone. Because I am the youngest, all of my siblings wanted to take care of me. But my money-smart brother spoke up and said, "You can stay in my home next week."

We all followed my money-dumb brother to his apartment. It was located downtown. We ate dinner together, and everyone enjoyed it. They asked me lots of questions about Americans such as, "Can you get along with Americans?" "Are American people nice?" "What kind of job are you working in?"

As my visit unfolded, the events and conversations revealed ten fallacies that people like my money-dumb brother have about money.

Fallacy #1: I Am Born Poor

After I answered all my siblings' questions, I told them that I liked the United States. It is a free country with nice, open-minded people. People there can achieve whatever they want based on their own abilities and ideas.

My money-dumb brother and I spoke privately during the week I spent with him. He told me he was broke because he had two sons to support and also had health problems. He complained a lot about the government. He was angry because it did not do anything to help him.

Because he was born poor, he felt he never did anything to become successful or achieve any goals. I remember him achieving some success though. When he was young, he was a leader in our town of more than 200 people. He finished high school too. Back then, someone who finished high school was considered an educated person. He also learned accounting by himself and became the first accountant in our town.

After the Chinese Cultural Revolution in the 1980s, he started his own business. He sold local goods to big cities, but he never earned good money from his business. Instead of blaming himself for creating an unprofitable business model, he just blamed the government and our parents. In reality, no one was born poor. It is everyone's birthright to be rich.

Fallacy #2: I'm Too Old or Too Young to Become Wealthy

He said, "Now I am too old to get started!" I told him, "No, you are not too old. People have started new businesses at fifty or sixty years old and went on to become wealthy." I told him the story of the founder of McDonald's.

Ray Kroc tried many business ideas when he was young. He found himself broke several times, but he never quit trying. He was fifty-two years old when he met the McDonald brothers in the 1940s. He marveled at the systems they used to prepare and serve food quickly. He suggested that they open more restaurants and became their exclusive franchising agent. His business launched McDonald's franchises throughout the country and later throughout the world. Ray Kroc is living proof that we are never too old or too young to get wealthy. But there is at least one advantage to being older — you have much more experience.

Fallacy #3: You Have to Quit Your Job and Start Your Own Business If You Want to be Rich

My money-dumb brother was well-known when he was young because he was the town leader. His job paid well, and his duty was to organize the labor of our townspeople. They worked in different farm fields producing rice and vegetables and also chopping and selling bamboo.

His job offered him a lot of opportunities to travel to different towns for meetings. He met many well-known leaders and businesspeople from other towns and counties during these trips. My family would sometimes host more than ten guests he had invited to town.

After more than twenty years in his government job, my money-dumb brother quit his job and started his own business. He believed if you want to get rich, you have to quit your job and start your own business. That belief is wrong. In fact, he would have been better off to stay in his government job because his business was not profitable.

There are other ways to get rich. One of the best ways is to save a portion of your income and invest it wisely. It allows you to build your wealth while maintaining a regular income flow from your current job. A lot of working-class people become rich just using their savings from their salaries.

Fallacy #4: You Can Get Rich Overnight

Allow me to dispel the rumors. There is no way to get rich overnight. There is no free lunch. We can't get something for nothing. We need to pay the price for getting knowledge or experience.

My money-dumb brother always tried to use his relationships with government officials to help him get big business deals, but he never succeeded. He told me a story about someone who had relatives or friends in the government. Because of his connections, that person got a big construction contract from the government and became a millionaire overnight. He also knew someone who got inside information from some contacts in the stock market. That person earned millions of dollars in just a few days during the stock market boom.

When I hear get-rich quick stories, I always have doubts. I don't believe overnight success exists. When people get money too quickly, they may not appreciate it or know how to handle it. They find their money disappears as quickly as it arrived.

Money is like a friend. You need to spend time with it, listen to its problems, and try to solve its problems with your own solutions. The more time you spend to earn money, the more you will appreciate it. Investing time and energy in a relationship ensures your friendships will not go bad. Treat your money the same way.

Fallacy #5: I Do Not Deserve to be Rich

Sometimes, my money-dumb brother would say, "I am not a very good person. I smoke and drink, and I have made a lot of mistakes in my life. That's why I am poor and never found success in life. God knows how bad I am, and He wants to punish me. I do not deserve anything better in my life."

You already have everything you need to succeed in life. You are born to be rich — no matter who you are, how poor you are, or where you are from. You have a birthright to be the best, and you deserve your own opportunity on this earth to be rich. Your right to be rich will never be denied, but you have to declare it and believe it is possible.

Fallacy #6: I Should Wait for Someone or the Government to Rescue Me

In China, when you work for the government or state-owned companies, you qualify for free meals, free housing, and even free transportation. The government also provides retirement benefits and health care. Sometimes my money-dumb brother would say, "Let's go talk to someone in the government to solve my problem."

I agreed that they might be able to help in some ways, but depending on them to solve all your problems is a flawed plan. Yes, sometimes the government may help you solve a small problem, but you will never get help with a major problem. There are just too many people waiting for the same limited government resources.

We can't wait for someone else or the government to rescue us and give us a boost on our road to success. If we do, we'll never get started, and we will be poor forever. When we depend on our own abilities, we have more control over our own life. You are the master of your own destiny.

Fallacy #7: Money Is Evil, and Rich People Are Bad

My money-dumb brother would say, "Money is evil. Rich people are not good, and they are so greedy." That is a big misconception about money and rich people. Money itself is not evil; it is just a sign of value. According to the Bible, the love of money is evil. Money is just a piece of paper. It only becomes powerful when someone uses it. If you use money for good, it will become a great help for humanity. If you use money for drinking, smoking, and drugs, it will destroy you.

Some people do not like Donald Trump because they think he is greedy, unkind, and stingy with his money. I have to admit I felt the same way. Later on, I changed my mind after learning about the Law of Attraction. Now when someone mentions Donald Trump, I picture him with beautiful golf course, beautiful cars, and his beautiful family. Then I say a prayer like this: "Thank you, Lord, for someone's mention of Donald Trump. Bless his beautiful golf course, bless his beautiful cars, bless his beautiful family, and bless his success." If you send out blessings, all good things will come back to you, and you will be blessed too.

Fallacy #8: The Economy Is Bad, So We Need to Wait

Newspapers and television news shows report bad news about the economy every day because that is the way the media operates. They use negative stories to catch people's attention. They make it sound like there are never any good days. All days have problems, and they concentrate on problems alone.

My money-dumb brother believes them: "This year, the economy is not good. No one has extra money to spend, so we have to wait until next year when everything turns around." You can't wait until the news reporters say the economy is good enough to start a business. Instead, please believe that there is no bad day for anything. Assume that every day is a perfect time to start something new or wonderful. Be ready to seize the opportunity at any time and at any moment.

Fallacy #9: It Is Useless to Save and Invest Money

It is a big mistake to avoid saving and investing money because of the risk of a stock market crash and inflation. It is impossible to work for money forever. We must save and invest so we can retire wealthy someday. Rich people never work for money; they let money work for them. Money has more energy than a human being. Plus, it does not need to sleep, eat, drink, or take a break. It can work twenty-four hours a day, seven days a week.

How much you can earn is less important than how much you can save and invest. You may have noticed that rich people become richer, and poor people become poorer. This happens because rich people utilize investing strategies to allow their money to grow. This frees them up to do other things.

On the other end of the scale, poor people need to work for their money because they spend everything they make. They lack a vision for a future as a rich person. This makes a big difference in a person's level of happiness. When we work for money, life feels tougher — like we can't make ends meet. We feel like we have fewer options because we need to work to survive.

The only way for regular people to step out of this negative cycle is to start saving — little by little, step by step. There is no shortcut. When you save money, you will have money to invest, and the money will earn or "attract" more money. It's another way we use the Law of Attraction to bring more success into our lives.

Fallacy #10: If I Borrow More Money, It Shows I Am More Important

Here is my money-dumb brother's last fallacy: If the bank can lend you more money, you will become a more important person. People use money to improve their status. Money can buy a big house and a nice car. Some people even borrow money from their credit cards to improve their credit score. It's unbelievable. Borrowing money makes you a slave, and the lender becomes your master.

Banks lend money to people because they want to earn money on the interest they charge. We already have to pay taxes, mortgage payments, and utilities that are part of normal living expenses. The less money we borrow, the more we can save. When we borrow too much money, it ensures we will be working for the bank forever. It also prevents us from saving anything, so we cannot make money work for us. To get started on the path to achieving financial independence, we have to stop borrowing money unnecessarily and start saving and investing.

Key Points in This Chapter

- We are not born poor. It is our birthright to be rich.
- We are never too young or too old to get rich.
- Saving and investing wisely is the best way to create wealth.
- It is almost impossible to get rich overnight.
- Everyone deserves to be wealthy.
- The best person to rely on is yourself.
- Money and the people who have it are not evil.
- There are many great opportunities, even in a poor economy.
- The sooner people save, the quicker money can grow.

知识创造财富

Ten Fallacies about Money

目标

Chapter 9
Your Financial Goals

"Effort fully releases its reward only after a person refuses to quit."
Napoleon Hill

I did not enjoy my time very much with my money-dumb brother. The second week, I stayed with my money-smart brother. He lives in a beautiful house. It has a small rose garden behind it and sits next to a scenic lake.

The conversation between my money-smart brother and I started with goals. My money-smart brother asked, "What are your specific goals in life?" I answered, "What do you mean by 'specific goals in life'?" He responded, "Such as how much money you want to earn in five years or ten years. What kind of position do you want to hold in the future? What do you want to do to help other people — give money or give your time?" I answered, "I do not have any specific goals for my life. I just want to be rich."

"I know everyone wants to be rich. But in order to get there, you need to have specific goals right now. If you do not have a specific goal, you will be lost. Based on my experience, I can tell you are broke now," he said. I asked, "How do you know I am broke now?" He answered, "Because you do not have any specific goals. People are always driven by goals. It's like driving a car without a map. You can't go anywhere if you do not know your destination."

What he said was true. I was very broke at that time. I strongly agreed with my money-smart brother's opinion about goals. I remembered several years earlier when I had a goal to complete my PhD. I worked day and night to achieve my goal. One class was terribly difficult and challenging. The class started out rough. There were endless homework and reading assignments. I also had to write several papers to submit to a referred journal. There were three mid-term tests, plus the final tests. The biggest challenge was to read more than ten papers and present five of them in the class.

I was scared to death of the first test in that doctorate class. The professor did not tell us any ranges, hints, or clues. All we could do to prepare for the test was to review ten whole chapters. The textbook was huge. Ten chapters amounted to about 200 pages. To make matters worse, I would have three different tests that same week. I tried to ask teachers to reschedule my test times, but I was not successful. Finally, I had to psyche myself up to face the challenge.

Having three tests in the same week required me to balance the time spent reviewing for the tests. That was a new challenge. Here is what I did to cope. I collected all the materials I had to review for the tests. Next, I wrote down all the time available to study that week in my planner. I divided each day into three time blocks: 8:00 a.m. to noon, 1:00 p.m. to 5:00 p.m., and 6:00 p.m. to 11:00 p.m. I scheduled time each day for the three classes in the available time periods.

The schedule was an important part of accomplishing my goal. I kept a calendar in my pocket. When one day passed, I used my pen to cross over that day on the calendar. That meant the day was forever gone. That would remind me to cherish the precious time. I had to work extra hard to use my time wisely.

My diligence paid off. I accomplished my goal of doing well on those tests. I used the same strategy to complete all the requirements for my PhD. My education ultimately helped me move from a poorly paid employee to a highly paid one.

When I was pondering my goals, my money-smart brother asked, "Do you want to know how to set up your goals?" I answered, "Of course, I would be glad to learn." He wrote this information on a piece of paper and handed it to me.

Financial goals in five years:

- A home worth $200,000
- A new BMW worth $50,000
- Bank account, cash, and other liquid assets worth $200,000
- A summer home in Florida worth $200,000
- Investments in the stock market and mutual funds worth $200,000
- Investments in real estate properties worth $200,000

Financial goals in ten years:

- A home worth $500,000
- A new BMW worth $100,000
- Bank account, cash, and other liquid assets worth $500,000
- A summer home in Florida worth $500,000
- Investments in the stock market and mutual funds worth $1,000,000
- Investments in real estate properties worth $1,000,000

Non-financial goals:

- Two-week vacations twice a year
- Associated with wealthy people in business and the arts
- A loving and charming wife and beautiful children
- A maid who handles cooking and cleaning

These goals seemed unattainable. My money-smart brother noticed the doubt on my face. "Do not worry how big your goal is. When you put your goals in writing, your subconscious mind will always search for the solutions," he said. Your subconscious mind will never sleep. It will always work hard for you. It has the connections with the highest intelligence."

"Of course, your goal should be a little realistic," he continued. "For example, earning a million dollars in five years is reasonable. Earning the first million dollars is tough. Once you have the first million though, the second million just needs two years, and the third million may just need one year."

He took out his wallet, and pulled out a very old check. I was surprised that he hung on to something like that. He told me the story of that old, barely recognizable check.

When he was twenty-two years old, he was very broke. He had just finished his military service after high school. He worked for a small company as a record keeper but could not make ends meet on his modest salary. One day while walking down the street, he saw a beautiful mansion. He had never seen such a stately home. He marveled at its huge yard. It was his dream house. There was a gate between him and the house, so he could only catch a glimpse.

A girl came out while he was looking at the house. He was stunned by her beauty. He had never seen such a lovely girl in his life. He wanted to speak to her, but he was afraid because he was so broke. When she left, he was still standing there. He thought the people who passed by suspected he had mental problems because he stood still for such a long time. But he did not worry about their strange looks.

That day was a turning point in his life. He realized he was nothing in the world. He had no money and no hope. Even his job was leading him nowhere. He saw that beautiful girl, but he didn't feel he could approach her. He wanted to change his life. He made a decision right then and there to marry that dream girl in five years.

After that, my money-smart brother went to a bank. He asked the teller if he could have a blank check because he wanted to open a bank account. He explained that he did not have his money with him, so he needed to have a blank check first. He would come back to deposit the money later on. The teller was confused by his request and refused to give him a blank check.

Unwilling to give up, he went to the manager. She was a nice, older lady. He told her that he just needed a blank check to keep because he had not seen one before. He promised he would become her customer later. There was a lot of competition in the banking business at that time. The manager saw he wasn't a bad person, so she gave him a blank check.

When he got home, he wrote his own name on the "Pay to the Order of" line on the check. He made the check out for $1,000,000. On the date line, he wrote a date that was exactly five years away. On the check's signature line, he wrote "God." He carefully tucked the one million dollar check into his wallet.

From then on, he was a totally different person. He decided to change his life by becoming a millionaire, so he could ask that girl for a date. But first, he needed an education. He knew he would never achieve his goal without it. He worked very hard at his job and finished early every day, so he would have time to study for the college entrance exam.

He studied day and night. After three months, he finished reviewing all his high school textbooks and passed the exams. He enrolled in an accelerated bachelor's degree program for adults. It would allow him to get a bachelors degree within two years if he worked hard enough. He was determined.

At first, he majored in Accounting. He studied one year and realized he should change his major to Finance. Back then, the stock market had just started in China. He thought he might have better opportunities with a degree in Finance. He met with his advisor and asked to change his major. His advisor told him that he had not encountered this situation before. Accounting was one of the most popular programs at their college. No one ever wanted to change majors because it was hard to get in the Accounting program. But my brother was persistent.

Finally, his advisor suggested he talk to the college president. My money-smart brother made an appointment and met with the president. The president was very nice and understanding. He was relieved when the president agreed to allow him to change his major to Finance. He knew he was now in control of his future.

After two years of study, he graduated with honors. Most graduates tried to find jobs in governmental departments or state-owned, established companies. He chose to work in a small bank. His classmates thought he was crazy, but he had his own ideas. He told his classmates that although that bank was small, the manager was highly educated and very open-minded. Besides that, the bank was growing very fast. Over the year he worked there, it quickly became a well-known regional bank.

That was in the 1980s. China had just opened its doors to the West, and the economy was booming. The first stock market had also just opened. It was unfamiliar to most people. No companies wanted to be listed in the stock market at first because no one understood what went on there.

My money-smart brother worked for a bank manager who was well-informed. His boss decided to be the first company listed in the Chinese stock market. Their company's initial public offering (IPO) was approved by the government after a lengthy process. It was hard to sell the stock because no one wanted it. Some people were reluctant to buy it because they really did not have any knowledge about the bank's stock. It didn't help that Hong Kong's stock market had just crashed. That made everyone cautious of the stock market.

Part of my brother's job was to sell $20,000 worth of stock. At that time in China, no one had much money. He had only sold $10,000 worth of his bank's stock after almost three months. He was frustrated and overwhelmed. If he could not meet his sales goal and sell $20,000 worth of stock, he would lose commission and maybe even his job. There was no way for him to sell the remaining $10,000 worth of stock despite his best efforts.

He decided he would buy it himself. He had just started his career, so he did not have any money. He borrowed money anywhere he could. He borrowed money from family members — $50 from his aunt, $100 from his uncle, $500 from his oldest brother, etc. It was tough to borrow such a huge amount, but he made it.

He worked hard at that bank and got promoted to manager of one of its branches. He learned from his experience, but he also craved new knowledge. And just as he believed, the stock market boomed. His stock performed very well. It split again and again. He never paid much attention to it since he bought the stock to keep. He used his salary to gradually pay back the money he borrowed from family members.

Time passed quickly. Before he knew it, he had been employed at the bank for almost three years. One day, he went to the bank's headquarters for a meeting. He saw a gorgeous girl in the credit department who looked very familiar. He couldn't remember where he met her. There was a party at the bank after the meeting. My brother saw the girl again. He said hello to her, and they started a conversation.

Suddenly, my brother realized she was the same girl he saw in front of that mansion five years earlier. Then, he realized it was exactly the same day of the same month as when he first saw her. He took out his wallet and found the million-dollar check he carried. He told the girl he needed to step away for a few minutes but would be right back.

He went downstairs and asked a bank teller to check his stock account. He never checked it before, so the teller asked him a lot of questions such as identification number, home address, etc. The teller was nice to him because he worked for the bank. Finally, the teller told my brother his stock was worth over $1,000,000. The stock market doubled almost every month, and his stock was worth more than 100 times what he originally paid for it.

He went upstairs and continued his conversation with the girl. He told her the story of the first time he saw her and how wanting to meet her inspired him to change his life. He explained how he wrote a check to himself, how he studied for his entrance exam so he could attend college, and how he got his first job. He went on to tell her about how he ended up buying $10,000 worth of stock so he could keep his job, and today he was a millionaire — all because of her.

The girl was moved by his amazing story. They started dating and became very close. They eventually got married.

Key Points in This Chapter

- Use goals as a road map for your life.
- Write down your goals in black and white.
- Decide what you want to do with your life and take control of your future.
- Accept new challenges every day.
- Always try your very best.
- Follow your dreams because dreams can come true.

知识创造财富

财富

Chapter 10
Seven Rules for Becoming Wealthy

"Do not follow where the path may lead.
Go instead where there is no path and leave a trail."
Muriel Strode

The story of my money-smart brother earning his first million and marrying his dream girl amazed me. He explained that being wealthy is a mind-set. "Did you know a lot of people win the lottery, but they eventually become poor again?" he asked. "Really? Why?" I answered. "Because they were poor and had a poor mind-set. They get rich quickly, so they do not learn how to deal with it. They spend money like it is an unlimited resource."

My brother continued, "We need to learn how to appreciate money and treat it as if it were a friend. Most people just use it. When we use our friends, they don't stick around very long. When money is treated as a friend, it becomes a lasting relationship. Managing money is a skill. Now I want to teach you seven rules of becoming wealthy."

Rule #1: It's Not How Much You Earn, but How Much You Save

We had a very poor relative. He went to the mountains one day and tried to plant some beans. He was shoveling dirt when suddenly, he heard a clanking sound. He was curious. He continued to dig and unearthed a big, old jar. He opened it to find thousands of old gold and silver coins inside.

He sold all the old gold and silver coins and became a millionaire overnight. The next day, he bought a $500,000 home with a 20 percent down payment. Immediately, he had to pay a huge commission, estate tax, city tax, and maintenance fees. Because the home was incredibly large, he had to hire two helpers. One helper handled cooking, cleaning, and care of the home's interior. The other one maintained the landscaping and exterior. Every day, lots of relatives and friends came over to ask for money. He would feed them and give them hundreds of dollars — just so they would leave.

Of course, he hired a financial advisor to manage his money and put some into the stock market. At the time, the stock market was down and the whole economy was struggling. He lost a fortune on his investment.

He made some bad choices too. He had an affair with a beautiful bartender and ended up divorcing his wife of twenty years. He married the bartender. They took a trip to Europe for their honeymoon. His new wife had expensive taste. He bought her new clothes and perfumes and whatever else she asked for.

After one year of his millionaire life, his new wife became unsatisfied and wanted a divorce. He had to pay a lawyer a huge amount of money to represent his case. He did not have much cash left for the legal fees, so he had to use stocks and bonds. Selling during a down market meant he took a huge loss on them. He ended up giving his home to his new wife in the divorce settlement and ended up with nothing. He was broke again.

Managing money is a skill. People who do not have this ability will never be rich. It is not how much you earn, but how much you save, that will determine your ultimate wealth. You need to save at least 10 percent of your income.

Rule #2: Pay Yourself First

Paying yourself first means that you deduct money for saving and investing before you spend your earnings on anything else. Most people do not use or even understand this concept. When most people receive a paycheck, they think of making debt, utility, and mortgage payments first.

Actually, the government receives the first payment. Taxes are deducted even before our paycheck leaves our company's payroll system. Regardless of how you feel about the value you get for the taxes the government deducts, you still have to pay Uncle Sam (a nickname Americans use for the government) first. FICA, social security, and federal, state, and local taxes provide important local services. Even though the United States government is the largest employer of Americans, citizens don't like big government because that means big taxes.

You work so hard; you deserve to keep part of your money. We have all experienced what happens when we do not intentionally set aside part of our paycheck for savings. We end up with nothing because there are always places to spend easily accessible money.

Everyone likes money and works for money, including the government. When you consider where money goes, it makes you realize how little you get from the money you earn. Your taxes alone are equal to about four or five months of earnings.

Then you work for credit lenders for four or five months — or maybe even the rest of the year. Lending institutions make money by charging interest on borrowed money. The more *you* borrow, the more *they* earn. Be cautious of the temptation to use credit cards.

Mortgage lenders offer borrowers the option for thirty-year mortgages, so they can borrow more money and purchase bigger homes. It's a much better idea for buyers to base their house payment budget on a fifteen-year mortgage.

I recall a two-thousand-year-old story about a young man in Babylon. He worked hard at his craft but was still very poor. He wanted to know why he couldn't accumulate any wealth. He worked on a project for a rich and wise man one day. When he finished, the wise man handed him the money he earned. The young man did not accept it. Instead, he asked the rich, wise man to teach him how to be rich.

The rich, wise man said poor people were poor because they did not know how to handle money. They just did their job, earned their wages, and spent their money. The young man was surprised by the answer. He asked why poor people do not know how to handle money. The rich, wise man explained that poor people want to learn to handle money correctly but may have never been taught. Some were taught, but the methods they learned did not work.

The wise man told him the number-one secret to becoming rich is to pay yourself first. The young man followed his advice. He began to save 10 percent of his wages as soon as he was paid. He spent the rest of his wages as usual. He felt a little uncomfortable in the beginning. He reduced his expenses over time and slowly adjusted to living on 90 percent of his wages.

He continued to learn from the rich, wise man. He invested his money in some businesses. He gave some money to a dealer he did not know. The dealer made a bad recommendation, so the young man lost his investment. But the rich, wise man encouraged him to keep trying. He assured the young man that it is okay to experience a loss on an investment as long as we learn from it.

The young man finally earned some money from his investments, but he spent his earnings on an extravagant celebration dinner. The rich, wise man told him that he just ate the interest. The young man was confused. He thought rich people should spend the money they earn. The rich, wise man told him that's one reason the poor stay poor.

Rich people save money and invest it so it can earn more money. Instead of working for money, they let money work for them. Poor people spend everything they make so their only choice is to work for more money. The rich, wise man instructed him to continue to save 10 percent of his wages. This time, he told the young man to reinvest the interest back into the total savings. The young man continued to learn to save, invest, and live wisely so he could accumulate wealth. Eventually, he became the richest man in Babylon.

We only can work eight to ten hours or maybe even twelve hours a day. We need the rest of the day to eat, relax, and sleep. Money doesn't need to rest like a human being. It can work twenty-four hours a day and seven days a week on our behalf to earn more money. Please remember to pay yourself first and take care of your money. Then, you can watch your money grow so it can take care of you.

Rule #3: The Power of Compound Interest

Suppose you have two job offers. One pays you $300 per day from the day you begin work. The other starts at $0.01, but your wages double every day you work. You are probably thinking, "That's crazy! Who would do a day's work for a penny?" Most people would choose the payment of $300 per day.

Let's take a closer look at the two payment scenarios. The first day, Job #1 pays $300, and Job #2 pays $0.01. The second day, Job #1 pays $300, and Job #2 pays $0.02. The third day, Job #1 pays $300, and Job #2 pays $0.04. As time goes on, Job #1 pays the same for a day's work, but the pay for Job #2 continues to double each day. Notice what happens in Table 1 on the next page. That's pretty amazing, isn't it?

Looking back now, a person who took Job #1 is probably thinking he made a big mistake. The person who was willing to take Job #2 only needed twenty-eight days to become a millionaire. That poor man who jumped at the $300 a day job would only have $8,400 at the end of the same time. That's an accelerated example of the way compound interest works. That's why Einstein said that compound interest is more powerful than a nuclear weapon.

Most people do not understand the power of compound interest rates. It looks like a small number, so they pay little attention to it. I've done the same thing in the past. I received a very good salary from my government job in China, but I did not know the power of compound interest. I put all my money in my checking account after I lost some money in the stock market. I was scared to death I would lose more money if I took a risk and invested it. So instead, I left my money sleeping in my checking account.

When we put money in a typical checking account, we lose money because of inflation. Right now, the inflation rate is about 4 to 5 percent

Table 1. The Power of Compound Interest

Day	The First Job		The Second Job	
	Payment	Total	Payment	Total
1	$300	$300	$0.01	$0.01
2	$300	$600	$0.02	$0.03
3	$300	$900	$0.04	$0.07
4	$300	$1,200	$0.08	$0.15
5	$300	$1,500	$0.16	$0.31
6	$300	$1,800	$0.32	$0.63
7	$300	$2,100	$0.64	$1.27
8	$300	$2,400	$1.28	$2.55
9	$300	$2,700	$2.56	$5.11
10	$300	$3,000	$5.12	$10.23
11	$300	$3,300	$10.24	$20.47
12	$300	$3,600	$20.48	$40.95
13	$300	$3,900	$40.96	$81.91
14	$300	$4,200	$81.92	$163.83
15	$300	$4,500	$163.84	$327.67
16	$300	$4,800	$327.68	$655.35
17	$300	$5,100	$655.36	$1,310.71
18	$300	$5,400	$1,310.72	$2,621.43
19	$300	$5,700	$2,621.44	$5,242.87
20	$300	$6,000	$5,242.88	$10,485.75
21	$300	$6,300	$10,485.76	$20,971.51
22	$300	$6,600	$20,971.52	$41,943.03
23	$300	$6,900	$41,943.04	$83,886.07
24	$300	$7,200	$83,886.08	$167,772.15
25	$300	$7,500	$167,772.16	$335,544.31
26	$300	$7,800	$335,544.32	$671,088.63
27	$300	$8,100	$671,088.64	$1,342,177.27
28	$300	$8,400	$1,342,177.28	$2,684,354.55

every year. That means when we don't invest our money, our money becomes less valuable.

Find ways to invest your money so it can grow. Never let it sleep.

Rule #4: Take Tax Advantages

The government imposes taxes on your income, but it also provides incentives to save. You have many options to save for retirement, an education for yourself and your kids, and even home mortgages. It's confusing, isn't it? You are probably wondering why the government does that.

The government wants you to get ahead, so you won't have to depend on Uncle Sam when you get older. Perhaps this is the first time you've heard about tax advantages the government offers. That's why this is the perfect time to study money. Accountants get paid well to know about tax advantages because many people do not know these tricks. They can be valuable allies to have on your side when it comes to saving money and avoiding excessive taxes.

There are several programs to help you get more out of your savings. First, the government provides tax incentives for contributing to your 401(k) retirement account. You do not pay tax on the money you contribute to your retirement account. That means you pay less tax overall. Many employers match 401(k) contributions as an added incentive. Employers have many different ways they handle matching. Some will match each dollar up to a certain amount, while others might match a percentage of everything employees contribute. Your human resources department will have more details if your company offers a 401(k) plan.

The benefit of a 401(k) is the ability to defer your taxes on the money you save. When you retire and begin to take the money out of your 401(k), you will still need to pay the tax. However, the tax rate at the time you retire may be less than it is while you are working, so you'll pay less in taxes overall.

The second tax incentive the government provides is for tax-deferred annuities. Like the 401(k), contributions to this type of annuity are not taxed until later. People who make a lot of money are usually in a higher tax bracket — that means they pay a larger percentage of their income to taxes. Investing in an annuity can reduce the total taxable income so the investor ends up in a lower tax bracket.

The tax advantages of these types of investments make a big difference in a person's net worth. Rich people get richer because they hire the best accountants and investment professionals to advise them, and they save money using tax-deferred methods. Poor people who don't follow the same wise practices just get poorer. They pay higher taxes on their income. Their job is taxed, their food is taxed, and their gas is taxed. Interestingly, people with wise saving and investing practices spend less money overall than poor people who save little or nothing. The poor tend to spend everything they earn on highly-taxed items.

A third incentive the government offers is a Roth IRA. It allows you to save money after tax. You can open a Roth IRA retirement account and invest up to $5,000 each year. When you take money out of your account during your retirement years, the growth part of money is tax-free. Think back to the chapter on compound interest. Over the twenty-, thirty-, or even forty-year life of a long-term investment, the growth of your investment will be significant. A Roth IRA allows you to hang on to all of the growth portion of your retirement funds.

Look at Table 2 on the next page to see what you can accumulate if you invest $5,000 each year at the average stock market return of 12 percent. It's pretty amazing what your $5,000 annual investment can do through the magic of compound interest. Investing $150,000 over thirty years, you can end up with $1,351,463. Perhaps the more amazing part is that the growth portion — $1,201,463 — is tax-free money at retirement.

Did you also notice that investing $5,000 each year at the average return of 12 percent would make you a millionaire in just twenty-eight years? That's why some people call the Roth IRA one of the best gifts from the government. Don't wait. Please take this opportunity to start your Roth IRA retirement investment as soon as possible.

The fourth government incentive works similarly to the Roth IRA.

Table 2. What a $5,000 Annual Investment Earns at a 12 Percent Return

Year	Investment		Interest		Total
	Current	Accumulated	Current	Accumulated	
1	$5,000	$5,000	$600	$600	$5,600
2	$5,000	$10,000	$1,272	$1,872	$11,872
3	$5,000	$15,000	$2,025	$3,897	$18,897
4	$5,000	$20,000	$2,868	$6,764	$26,764
5	$5,000	$25,000	$3,812	$10,576	$35,576
6	$5,000	$30,000	$4,869	$15,445	$45,445
7	$5,000	$35,000	$6,053	$21,498	$56,498
8	$5,000	$40,000	$7,380	$28,878	$68,878
9	$5,000	$45,000	$8,865	$37,744	$82,744
10	$5,000	$50,000	$10,529	$48,273	$98,273
11	$5,000	$55,000	$12,393	$60,666	$115,666
12	$5,000	$60,000	$14,480	$75,146	$135,146
13	$5,000	$65,000	$16,817	$91,963	$156,963
14	$5,000	$70,000	$19,436	$111,399	$181,399
15	$5,000	$75,000	$22,368	$133,766	$208,766
16	$5,000	$80,000	$25,652	$159,418	$239,418
17	$5,000	$85,000	$29,330	$188,749	$273,749
18	$5,000	$90,000	$33,450	$222,198	$312,198
19	$5,000	$95,000	$38,064	$260,262	$355,262
20	$5,000	$100,000	$43,231	$303,494	$403,494
21	$5,000	$105,000	$49,019	$352,513	$457,513
22	$5,000	$110,000	$55,502	$408,014	$518,014
23	$5,000	$115,000	$62,762	$470,776	$585,776
24	$5,000	$120,000	$70,893	$541,669	$661,669
25	$5,000	$125,000	$80,000	$621,670	$746,670
26	$5,000	$130,000	$90,200	$711,870	$841,870
27	$5,000	$135,000	$101,624	$813,494	$948,494
28	$5,000	$140,000	$114,419	$927,914	$1,067,914
29	$5,000	$145,000	$128,750	$1,056,663	$1,201,663
30	$5,000	$150,000	$144,800	$1,201,463	$1,351,463

The government allows you to invest in an education for you or your kids by creating an educational fund account. The growth in the fund is tax-free like the Roth IRA. The annual contribution limit for the educational fund is $2,000. If you start early, the growth part of your investment will be enormous, and it also will be tax-free. A fully funded education for your children is in your hands.

The government offers other tax incentives such as the ability for homeowners to deduct mortgage interest and real estate taxes. People who are self-employed and have a home office have additional tax incentives. For instance, they can write off a portion of their home's maintenance expenses.

Business ownership, even for people who work for a company, can be a good way to invest money and receive tax incentives. That's why rich people often own companies. They hire accountants to help them take advantage of tax incentives and pay fewer taxes.

Rule #5: Don't be a Slave to Debt

Borrowing money makes you a slave, and the lender becomes your master. Never borrow money for anything but necessities, such as an education or home mortgage. One book I read suggested that one of the best money management strategies is to avoid borrowing money altogether. If you borrow money, you have to pay interest, and you will be working for someone else. A lot of people never get ahead in their lives because they borrow too much money. It causes them to spend the rest of their lives owing interest to lenders.

Borrowing money from credit card companies usually means high interest rates. Some interest rates are as high as 20 or 30 percent. Money management expert and talk show host Dave Ramsey tells his radio listeners to cut up their credit cards and throw them away.

Rule #6: Dollar Cost Average Investing

People often think they need a large sum of money to invest in the stock market or mutual funds. Most of us do not have that kind of money. Instead, we just let our money sit in a savings account. Here is good news — dollar cost average investing is one of the best investment strategies for common people. In dollar cost averaging, we contribute to an investment account on a regular basis to purchase shares of mutual funds. Because we are buying a little at a time, it reduces the chance of buying shares at the wrong time.

One of the challenges we face for investing is timing. Many factors affect share prices, and they can fluctuate wildly. Because investors are sometimes impulsive, they think about getting into the market when the price of stocks or mutual funds is high. When the price is low and the market is bad, they want to sell the stock and funds and get out of the market. The irony is that it is a good time to buy when the market is bad and the price is low.

Dollar cost averaging can reduce the uncertainty of investment timing. We need to invest a planned amount of money at specific time intervals to buy mutual funds. When the price is high, you buy. When the price is low, you also buy. You will eventually get the average cost of total investment and achieve the average earnings of the stock market (the U.S. stock market's average earning is 10 to 12 percent in the long run).

Rule #7: Don't Put All Your Eggs in One Basket

Diversifying your investments will reduce your risk. Don't put all your eggs in one basket. Select mutual funds with a good track record of winning for more than five years, preferably for more than ten years. Don't look at their one-year or three-year track records because you need to think long term. Spread your retirement investing evenly across four or five types of funds. Here is a good example:

- Allocate 25 percent of your investment to growth and income funds (sometimes called large cap or blue chip funds).

- Allocate 25 percent of your investment to growth funds (sometimes called mid cap or equity funds; an S&P Index fund would also qualify).

- Allocate 25 percent of your investment to international funds (sometimes called foreign or overseas funds).
- Allocate 25 percent of your investment to aggressive growth funds (sometimes called small cap or emerging market funds).

Key Points in This Chapter

- It is not how much you earn, but how much you save.
- Set money aside for saving as soon as you receive your paycheck.
- Money that is left alone to earn compound interest can grow surprisingly fast.
- The government wants you to save for retirement and offers incentives that reduce your taxes.
- Borrowing money makes you a slave to a lender.
- Set aside a pre-determined amount of money on regular intervals to invest. Using dollar cost average investing will reduce the possibility of buying your investments at a bad time.
- Protect your future by choosing a variety of different types of investments.

知识创造财富

成功

Chapter 11

An Investing System That Never Fails

*"Most fear in life comes from lack of knowledge;
seldom from any real threat."*
Charles Givens

I was very excited about the seven rules of money that my money-smart brother taught me, but investing was still a challenge. Nevertheless, I knew it was time for me to learn to invest.

I had not had good luck with my investments over the years. I bought 1,000 shares of stock when I worked for the Chinese government as an assistant economist. The price of that stock increased more than 10 percent in just a month. Shortly thereafter, a friend of mine told me about the sudden death of a Chinese leader – Deng Xiaoping. He was one of the most important people in China because he maintained peace with other nations. My friend believed the stock market would crash after his death. I listened to his advice and sold all my stock. Much to my surprise, the result was quite the opposite: the price nearly doubled after a few days.

I had a job where I was secure and well paid, but I was broke. I was ignorant about how to manage my own money even though I had a bachelor's degree in Accounting and a master's degree in Finance. Formal education unfortunately doesn't cover how to manage personal finances, save, and plan for retirement. That's why a lot of well-educated people retire with no money. Sadly, only 15 percent of retirees have enough money to cover their daily expenses. It was not until I received a job offer to teach at a college in 2006 that I realized I needed to learn how to manage my own money.

I decided to learn everything I could about money management and investing. I read popular investment books, attended seminars, and invested in the stock market and mutual funds. I read over 100 books which included biographies, financial achievement, and motivation. I was still not sure about investing and managing money, so I read more books. Eventually I read more than 200 books, but I finally became excited about discovering the secrets of personal achievement and investing.

Based on what I learned in those books, I invested my retirement and other savings in mutual funds. Unfortunately, the stock market crashed in 2008. It destroyed my basic concept of investing, and I lost half of the value of my investments. I was shocked; I thought I knew how to invest. I sympathized with a lot of people who had the same experience I did.

After that horrifying event, I sought the advice of my money-smart brother. He became a self-made millionaire by investing in the stock market when he was twenty-seven years old. My brother shared the secret of his investment success with me. Based on his advice, I sold all my mutual funds and bought several stocks.

His system worked for me, and I was thrilled. Now I want to share my brother's never-fail investing system with you. Many people who invest in the stock market lack sufficient financial knowledge. It can make you feel uncertain and cause you to worry about the stock market since your hard-earned money is invested there. When the market goes up, you feel ecstatic. When the market goes down, you feel extremely sad. The market is like the weather: You never know what will happen the next day, even with good forecasting. If you can't tolerate the uncertainty, quit buying stocks.

Knowledge is the central part of this winning investing system. This system helped my brother become a millionaire. It also helped me become financially independent. More than five of my relatives have become wealthy using this investing system. It will help you too.

How to Choose a Stock

Before we discuss the never-fail investing system, we first need to answer a pertinent question: how can I find a good stock?

A key element of this investing system is to find a good stock at a good price. A good stock is usually a company with a good management team. The company provides a good product or service that is in high demand.

Good Price

You ultimately want to buy a stock at a discounted price (less than 50 percent is perfect). To accomplish this, you can calculate the expected value of each stock.

Good Management

A company needs a strong leadership team with outstanding management skills. You can research each of the team members' credentials, experiences, and achievements, as well as any negative news about them. Based on the news and the quality of the individual members, you can judge the quality of the management team and their ability to lead the company.

Some evidence of a good management team is a company with a good debt-to-asset ratio (less than 0.5) and good cash flow (growing every quarter for the last five years). You can find these two accounting numbers in their annual reports or on their websites. If these numbers are poor, the company could not withstand an economic crisis. The company would have limited ability to repay debt. As a result, it couldn't pass through a crisis.

Good Product or Service

The company should provide a good quality product or service that is useful and meaningful. For example, a car is useful and it can take you where you need to go. The quality of a car is a good measure of the car's price. Japan's ability to produce a quality product has positioned Japan as a powerful economic nation. Similarly, I bought

Netflix stock because their online movie rental service makes sense, and everyone likes the way the company operates its business.

Good Market Demand

There must be high demand for the product or service in the marketplace. The quality of the product or service is important. However, the availability of consumers who want to buy or use the product or service is of greater importance.

Several key accounting numbers deserve your attention: sales, revenue, and profit. These are the three numbers you can find on many Internet websites, such as www.yahoo.com and www.CNN.com. Over the last five to ten years, companies worth investing in should show at least a 15 percent increase each year. Never invest when these numbers are negative. For example, if the profits are negative, it shows the business cannot earn money. You would just throw your money away.

Evaluating a Stock's Earnings

To get started, you must first gather the company's earnings per share (EPS) figures. You then take this number and divide it by the annual return on investment you are comparing it with (discount rate). For example, if X stock has $5 in earnings per share and you want to compare it with 5 percent treasury bonds, you simply divide $5 by .05 to get $100 (the intrinsic value of X stock).

That example only takes into consideration the stock's current earnings. If you are interested in finding out what the stock will theoretically be worth next year, you just substitute next year's expected EPS with the current one. So if X stock is expected to earn $10 per share next year, you divide 10 by .05. It will give you an intrinsic value of $200, relative to government bonds.

Now that you know what the stock is worth, you can compare its current stock price with its intrinsic value to decide if it is worth the risk. For example, if X was trading at $45, you would consider it undervalued because it is trading at a price that is less than $100.

However, if it was trading at $120 per share, it would be considered overvalued.

When to Buy Stock

The stock market can be a gambling game. People without enough knowledge will probably lose money or break even, just like at a casino. That's why casinos lure you with attractive deals on rooms, food, and entertainment, as well as free alcohol. The owners know you will eventually lose money.

I learned this lesson when I was a child. My mom liked card games. She bet with a very small amount of money, but that sum of money seemed very large to me back then. We gambled almost every day during the holidays. At that time, I was ignorant and knew nothing about gambling. Sometimes I put all my chips into one game, and I usually lost all my money. I learned a hard lesson that I remembered my entire life.

I learned my lesson during childhood and never gambled as an adult. I know I will never win the game and will always break even or lose money. Why should I waste my time? But with this successful investing system, you know the rules for timing stock purchases. It won't be a gamble at all.

You can buy and sell any time you need based on your knowledge of the stock market. Most people make the mistake of buying stock when the price goes up, and they sell when the price goes down. No one knows when the price is at its lowest level or highest level, so everyone just gambles. Even with sophisticated computing software, no one really knows how the market will behave.

Avoid the dangerous guessing game, and do your homework. Investigate the company to see if it is a good time based on the market demand for the product or service and the quality of the management team. If you feel uncertain based on those numbers, follow your instinct and don't buy it. If you receive information that a particular stock is a good bargain, buy it at the current price. The market price will eventually merge with your expected value, which will give you a profit.

In this systematic way, the whole stock market game turns out to be easy. You do not need to look at the stock market every day. Even stock market crises provide opportunities to buy low, discounted stocks, which will earn even more profit.

How Long to Hold Stocks

When we buy stocks, it is natural to worry about the price fluctuating up or down. Because we do not know what will happen next, we feel uncertain. If the price goes down and we think the market is going bad, it is tempting to immediately sell our stock. But if we sell and the market surprises us and goes up, we are left with regret.

People often act out of emotional fear rather than knowledge. Knowledge is power. Recall the formula where we calculated the expected value. When you know your expected value, you can rest assured that the market will eventually merge the market price with the expected value. Have faith in the market. Hold your stock until the price goes up or exceeds your expected value. Once it does, it is time to sell it for a profit.

This process makes playing the stock market game simple and automatic. You do not need to let the uncertainty of today's stock price bother you. In the long term, you will not lose money if you are patient and avoid selling out of fear.

Armed with knowledge about the stock, you will never worry about your money. You will be confident that the market price will ultimately go up and satisfy your expectations. But be patient! Sometimes it takes a very long time for the market price to merge with your expected value.

How to Handle Inside Information

This winning investing system focuses on the fundamental analysis and true value of stocks. It eliminates the need for any other information, including inside information. When you finally get it, it is probably no longer inside information.

If you buy and sell based on this so-called inside information, you probably will go in the opposite direction of the market. The big guys, such as mutual fund companies and big investors, have already done the buying and selling. It is most likely too late for you. Additionally, inside information can lead you astray — especially if you don't have basic knowledge on the value of your stock. Insiders are not experts, and they cannot predict the future. Listening to them might lead you in the wrong direction.

I started this chapter with the story of my first stock-trading experience when I worked at the job in China. My friend had some information about the death of Deng Xiaoping and advised me to sell my stock. I sold all my stock; however, the market went up instead, and the price of my stock doubled. I lost a big opportunity because I listened to that false prediction. If I had not received that information, I would have held that stock and earned a huge profit. Please learn from my mistake.

The System Works

Remember the story in Chapter 9 about how my money-smart brother, who is five years older than me, became wealthy? He invested in the stock market based on this investing system and became a millionaire.

Here is how the system worked for him. It was the 1980s, and he was twenty-two years old. He went to college and landed a job with a bank after he graduated two years later. The bank's business took off after he started working there. It became the first business to list stock in the Chinese stock exchange. Because he worked there, he knew their service was excellent, there was good market demand for the services, and the management team was great.

As part of his job, my brother was obliged to sell the bank's stocks to customers. He worked hard and sold most of his obliged shares. But he couldn't sell the last 1,000 shares. He decided to buy them so he would not lose his job. He raised the money to buy the shares by borrowing $10,000 from his friends, colleagues, family members, and relatives.

The stock market took off and the price of his stock grew — five times, ten times, twenty times. He heard rumors every day the stock price was too high, the market would crash, and their stocks would become meaningless pieces of paper. Stockholders started selling their stocks. They were earning huge profits at the time so they were satisfied that they made the right decision. My brother did not need the money right away, so he did not sell his stock.

Finally, three years after he started working at the bank, the price of his bank's stock was up 100 times from the original price. He became a self-made millionaire at just twenty-seven years old. It was an amazing story that validates the investing system. Even though it was accidental at the time, he analyzed the process and has used it in other stock purchases.

Let's recap what he did. He knew it was a good stock at a good price. He had faith in the company's services, market, and management team. He bought the stock at a low price and held on to his stock so it could reach its expected value. He followed the fundamentals and ignored wayward advice from others. Finally, he sold his stock and became a millionaire. This investing system can be a powerful tool you can use to achieve your financial independence as well.

Key Points in This Chapter

- Do your homework on the company. Assess the market demand for the product or service and the quality of the management team.
- Have faith in the market.
- Disregard inside information.

知识创造财富

成就

Chapter 12

You Can Achieve Whatever You Want

*"Progress always involves risk; you can't steal second base
and keep your foot on first base."*
Fredrick Wilcox

My money-smart brother asked, "Why do some people succeed and some fail? What makes a successful person different from those who fail?" I answered, "I don't know." He went on to explain the traits of successful people. As he listed them, I realized I had seen those in successful people I knew. It raised my awareness as I met more people.

You may not realize that most millionaires and other successful people started from nothing. Some of them experienced failure and had to start over several times. One example is Donald Trump. He once owed billions of dollars to banks before he recovered and became a billionaire again. Many great men in history were self-made, including Napoleon Bonaparte, Benjamin Franklin, and Abraham Lincoln.

I have read many personal development books, conducted extensive research, and attended seminars taught by motivational experts like Tony Robbins and Brian Tracy. They all seem to agree on several basic rules for people who want to succeed. These rules are crucial for those who seek to achieve success in every area of life — financial, physical, mental, and spiritual wellness. Most importantly, these rules will help you maintain peace of mind. Read on for the rules.

Be Willing to Learn

The most prominent quality successful people possess is a willingness to learn. Anyone can succeed in life if he or she is willing to learn. Education alone can help you achieve any result. You can learn about anything — issues regarding your career, family, finances, and health — *only if you want to*! Learning is an intentional, lifelong process.

People usually think of education as the knowledge we learn in the classroom. School learning is only a small part of the educational process. We also have to include real-life experiences, books, on-the-job training, self-taught knowledge, and learning from other people — historical figures and people we know. Many people think graduation from school means you finished learning, but it's quite the opposite. A commencement ceremony happens at the end of our high school or college education, but commencement is actually a beginning. When you graduate from college, you start the learning process of life.

Of course, learning is not easy! It requires tremendous effort, and that's why a lot of people fail. But the good news is that anyone can learn and everything is learnable. Never stop learning. If you stop learning, your growth stops. Every day is a new day, a risk, or an adventure, and you never know what the next step will bring. That is what makes life so interesting. If you already know what the next step is, where is the excitement? Every day brings new challenges, and we must work to find the solutions. That is why knowledge is the most powerful thing in the world, and everyone wants to get it.

Most importantly, education can help you open your mind and accept different ideas. Ignorance is a major factor in poverty, disease, crimes, and hopeless situations. Most social problems can be solved through education.

In my career, I've spent a lot of time with college students. Some of my students said they could not learn and my classes were too tough. Here is the truth: They were not willing to learn. **If there is a will, there is a way.** The first step toward personal and financial success should be to adopt a lifelong-learner mind-set. All individuals have the ability and the capacity to learn. If you don't believe this, consider the process you used to learn to walk. After a few failed attempts, you succeeded. Learning is a process that involves trial and error. Understanding that will help you feel better about taking some risks.

Believe in yourself. Before attempting something new, say to yourself, "**I will, I will, and I will.**" A positive mind-set will influence your subconscious mind and override negativity that is present. Over time, you will make the first important step toward your goal — becoming a lifelong learner.

Create a Healthy Lifestyle

If you want to succeed in life, you need to reduce distractions. What do you think is the worst distraction you'll encounter on the road to personal and financial success? It isn't living in a poor neighborhood. It isn't having a poor family or friends. It is poor health.

I recently read that one-third of Americans are overweight or have diabetes. The medical costs are $150 billion each year. Ten years from now, the medical costs for diabetes will have doubled. Did you know that most health-related problems such as heart disease, diabetes, and cancer are preventable in most cases? They can obviously be treated with medicine once they occur, but they can also be prevented by eating a proper diet, exercising, and avoiding bad habits such as smoking or drinking.

Consider physical fitness a basic necessity for achieving success in every area of your life. These mostly preventable diseases cause pain and suffering. The associated hospital bills will create a nightmare as well. This is why most developed western countries provide universal health care. They want poor or underprivileged people who get sick to be able to get treatment without having to worry about the cost of hospital bills.

Since health care reform is a hot topic in the United States, people may think that getting sick is okay because the government will pay the medical bills. But there is much more to illness than just medical expenses. Once you become ill, there is no easy fix. Illness can cause problems in your career, relationships, and peace of mind. Prevention is better than correction.

I recently read a book called *Nurtured by Love: The Classic Approach to Talent Education* by Shinichi Suzuki. Mr. Suzuki was from an influential family. His father was the founder of the largest violin factory in the world. At age thirty-five, the author was diagnosed with a stomach disease. He visited famous doctors around the world. His family spent a lot of money and tried desperately to find someone who could cure the disease. It appeared there was no way for him to survive. Giving up, he waited in his bed to die in peace.

One day, an old Chinese traditional medical doctor visited him and provided a simple prescription: **only eat soup and vegetables**. Mr. Suzuki followed the instructions. One week later, he was out of his death bed. His vitality eventually returned, and he enjoyed a quality life. He lived to be ninety-nine years old.

Exercise Self-Discipline

Self-discipline or self-control is one of the top traits of successful people. People are not born with it! Self-discipline is acquired through training. Every religion and tribe has tried to develop a system to help people succeed in life.

For example, monks in a monastery get up early in the morning, eat only vegetables, read the sacred books, and practice martial arts every day. Most of the temples were built on top of mountains. They are far away from crowded places so the monks can experience solitude. This allows them to almost forget their physical existence and achieve spiritual peace.

Meditation works the same way. You need to go to a quiet place and sit without any disturbance so you can meditate in the presence of your inner peace. For me, before studying or doing important activities, I find a quiet place, lie down, and close my eyes. I lie quietly for a while or take a power nap. Sometimes just five minutes totally reenergizes me. Even when your life feels out of control, you can take charge and become the captain of your destiny. All it takes is a few minutes of solitude.

Take Responsibility for Your Actions

In my career as an educator, I encounter students who fail my classes because they never show up or never work hard enough to help themselves. Students sometimes think the teachers should be held responsible for the students' studies. But quite the opposite is true. Some students never understand they are the ones who should be responsible for their studies and their own destiny. People who rely on someone else — parents, school, or government — to determine their future never succeed in life.

We must take responsibility for our life. No one knows better than you what's really going on in your life. Some students think their parents will provide money to pay for school, take care of their living expenses, and help them find a good job. That may be true, but students have to do their part: study hard in school, earn good grades, work hard in their jobs to advance and earn money, and take care of themselves and their future. Eventually, their parents will not be by their sides, and they will only have themselves to depend on.

Students need to be responsible for their studies. Once they fail a class, it is too late to get help. If they feel themselves slipping, they should seek guidance immediately. They need to take responsibility for communicating with teachers to find out what the problems are. Then, they need to work hard and seek help from others if needed. Only by taking responsibility for their learning, can they achieve success in school. And that isn't a practice just for students. Taking responsibility for all areas of life can help everyone overcome obstacles.

No matter what shape the economy is in, we need to take responsibility for our own finances. Some people think the government will take care of them when they are old. If this is you, please wake up right now! If we wait for the government to save for us, we will never get ahead in life. Research shows that in ten years, social security funds will be negative. That means the government **can not** pay for our retirement.

This means we need to take care of our own money. We need to learn how to invest, save for retirement, and analyze potential tax advantages. Never put your hard-earned money completely into someone else's hands. Even if you have a financial advisor, you should always know what they are doing with your money. No one is more interested than you in protecting your money and making it grow. So talk to your financial advisor, ask questions, learn all you can about your money, take full responsibility for your finances, and control your own destiny.

Show Gratitude Every Day

One thing that baffles me as an educator is how some students don't appreciate having someone pay for his or her tuition. It does not matter whether the family or the government is paying, the student often does not make good grades. Students often don't realize how hard it is to earn every dollar. They think money is easy to get and there is plenty of free money available.

They are lucky to have good parents or a good government. However, they sometimes don't realize there are millions of people who do not have food to eat or clothes to wear. It is sad to see parents work hard to save money so their children can attend school when it results in their children's lack of awareness. The children end up thinking their education is free, and they do not appreciate the effort.

Every success in life has its own price. If you want to achieve success, you have to pay your own way. Even if someone has already paid for you, you still have to work hard to achieve your own success. Achieving success in life is not easy. Showing sincere appreciation helps students realize how lucky or blessed they are to have someone paying their tuition or costs. We must concentrate on working hard to achieve our goals in life.

The Law of Attraction suggests that we will get in life what we give. If you send out blessings, you will receive blessings. If you send out positive information, you will receive positive results. If you send out appreciation, you will receive more help in your life, people will appreciate your efforts, and the whole world will smile at you.

Maybe you have bad parents, bad neighbors, bad relationships, bad jobs, or bad days. Avoid the urge to complain about them. Complaining will never solve your problems. Instead, count your blessings and the good things that happen in your life. Even if you feel like you have nothing to be thankful for, just be thankful for your biological parents who gave birth to you. Every morning when you get up, express gratitude for a beautiful new day. Then thank your family, employers, and everyone who helps you. When you encounter other people, flash them a smile. With this type of attitude, you will be sure to have many great days ahead.

Be Specific about What You Want and Write It Down

Most of us are busy with our jobs, families, and other duties. We don't have time to think about what we really want from life. Even if we know what we want, we rarely take the time to write specific things on paper. However, if we do not know what we want, we will drift aimlessly in life. It is like a ship in the ocean. It can't go anywhere if the captain does not know the destination.

Please take time to think about your life. Write down your goals — long term and short term — and be specific. Once you do that, write down the actions you should take to achieve these goals. If the results are not what you expected, think of ways to adjust your goals or modify your actions to reach your destination.

Being specific means making realistic goals that you can feel, touch, and smell. It is not specific enough to say, "I want a beautiful car." You need to say, "I want to own a BMW convertible in five years." Go to the BMW dealer to drive that dream car, so you can easily visualize yourself driving that car in five years. Ask the dealer for a car brochure so you can hang the pictures in your home where you can see them every day. That way, you won't forget what you are working for.

Set goals for every area of your life — career, family, finances, and relationships. For example, actor Jim Carrey wrote a million-dollar check to himself when he was broke and had no job. He told himself he would receive a million-dollar job offer in five years. Then, he worked hard and finally succeeded. He is one of the biggest names in Hollywood today.

Determine What You Want

An essential part of achieving success is determining what you really want. You can only plan the next step to success if you have goals in mind. It is like leaving for a trip without any idea where you want to go and a plan for getting there.

A lot of students fail college and high school. As a college professor, I noticed the school systems only teach students the material in the textbooks. They rarely help them with necessary skills or techniques to achieve success in life.

I understand the difficulty most people experience when getting an education because I experienced numerous challenges getting my own. That inspired me to help poor or underprivileged students. To show my commitment, I wrote this book about how to achieve the dream of attaining success. My ultimate goal is to help all individuals discover their potential and realize that they can achieve anything they want in life.

Take Action and Pay the Price

A goal without action means nothing. **To achieve your goal, you need to take action. You can't have something for nothing.** Once you determine your goal, create a strategy for achieving that goal. Do you need training or education? Can you learn what you need by reading? Do you need experience? Changing jobs or volunteering for a charity can give you the experience you need.

It will never be too late to start. You are never too old or too young to take action to achieve your dreams. But you need to start somewhere. Do not just wait for it to come. Even if there is nothing to start with, just go out and look for any kind of job you can find, and start to work toward your goals right now! Only work can give you confidence, self-esteem, and self-reliance. Work can also keep you busy so you don't have time for negative thoughts. Additionally, you can make new friends, change your environment, and launch your new life.

Research shows that people who don't maintain active lives after retirement reach their death faster. They quit making goals and find themselves with nothing to strive for. Everyone should create an active life. We all need dreams — something to hope for. When we lose hope, there is no point in living. Please never give up on your dreams. Sometimes you need to take risks. It may be scary, but it is worth it to try. This is what makes life interesting and fun. Even when we make mistakes or fail, we grow.

I once tried to find a roommate. One guy contacted me. We talked for a while, and I got to know him a little bit. He had a car accident ten years earlier and suffered brain damage. The government was now paying him about $800 per month, so he felt he no longer needed to work. I asked what he did every day. He spent most of his time watching television. Sometimes, he would go to the hospital to see the doctors. He looked like a normal person, and I did not see any problems with him. I asked why he did not try to find a job or something to do. He said he would lose the $800-a-month disability payment the government gave him if he got a job, and he didn't want that to happen. I was shocked.

He did not own a car. He did not even know how to use a computer. He said he did not need a car since the government would send a car for the disabled when he needed to go shopping or to the hospital. He felt he could not learn to use a computer because he was disabled. He believed the government gave him money because he could not learn. Besides, if he received training, the government would expect him to get a job, and he would lose his disability money.

I thought that was pathetic. How could a grown man spend the rest of his life just watching television? He was only thirty years old and had given up on life. Never give up or sell your life short, no matter what the circumstances are. There's always a way out.

Never Give Up

Only people with persistence and determination achieve an extraordinary life. Abraham Lincoln was one of the greatest American presidents. He was well-known for his determination, persistence, and never-give-up spirit despite numerous failures. Here is a time line of the major parts of his life. Notice how many setbacks he had.

1831	Lost his job
1832	Defeated in the race for Illinois State Legislature
1833	Failed in business
1834	Elected to Illinois State Legislature
1835	Sweetheart died
1836	Had a nervous breakdown
1838	Defeated in the race for Illinois House Speaker
1843	Defeated for the nomination for U.S. Congress
1846	Elected to Congress (success)
1848	Lost re-nomination to Congress
1849	Rejected for land officer position
1854	Defeated in the race for U.S. Senate
1856	Defeated for the nomination for Vice President of the United States
1858	Again defeated in race for U.S. Senate
1860	Elected President of the United States

Success Is Yours to Achieve

Just like my money-smart brother, you can achieve whatever you want in life as long as you have a system. In previous chapters, we (my money-smart brother, my money-dumb brother, and I) shared our mistakes and lessons with you so you can learn from them. We provided practical steps you can take to achieve your financial independence. I communicated important skills and techniques you will need to overcome obstacles on your journey to personal and financial success.

You were born with the highest potential. With hard work and a willingness to learn, you can make the most out of your life. I have given you all the tools I can. The rest is up to you. Please choose to take action right now. My money-smart brother achieved his financial independence, I am achieving my financial independence, and you can achieve your financial independence too.

知识创造财富

You Can Achieve Whatever You Want

Recommended Books

- *The Instant Millionaire* by Mark Fisher (New World Library, 1993)
- *The One-Minute Millionaire* by Mark Victor Hansen and Robert Allen (Three Rivers Press, 2009)
- *Think and Grow Rich* by Napoleon Hill (Random House Publishing Group, 1987)
- *The Richest Man in Babylon* by George S. Clason (Signet, 2004)
- *Secrets of the Millionaire Mind* by T. Harv Eker (Harper Business, 2005)
- *The Greatest Salesman in the World* by Og Mandino (Bantam, 1983)
- *The Millionaire Next Door* by Thomas J. Stanley and William D. Danko (Pocket, 1999)
- *The Science of Getting Rich* by Wallace D. Wattles (Thinking Stuff LLC, 2007)
- *Rich Dad Poor Dad* by Robert T. Kiyosaki and Sharon L. Lechter (Business Plus, 2010)
- *Awaken the Giant Within* by Anthony Robbins (Free Press, 1992)
- *You Were Born Rich* by Bob Proctor (Life Success Pacific Rim, 2003)
- *See You at the Top* by Zig Ziglar (Pelican Publishing, 2000)
- *7 Strategies for Wealth & Happiness* by Jim Rohn (Three Rivers Press, 1996)
- *Creating Wealth* by Robert G. Allen (Free Press, 2006)
- *The Millionaire Mind* by Thomas J. Stanley (Andrews McMeel Publishing, 2001)
- *Little Red Book of Selling* by Jeffrey Gitomer (Bard Press, 2004)
- *The Automatic Millionaire* by David Bach (Crown Business, 2005)

- *Rule #1* by Phil Town (Crown Business, 2007)
- *The Wealthy Barber* by David Chilton (Prima Lifestyles, 1996)
- *The Total Money Makeover* by Dave Ramsey (Thomas Nelson, 2009)
- *The 9 Steps to Financial Freedom* by Suze Orman (Three Rivers Press, 2006)
- *21 Success Secrets of Self-Made Millionaires* by Brian Tracy (Berrett-Koehler Publishers, 2001)
- *Cracking the Millionaire Code* by Mark Victor Hansen and Robert Allen (Harmony, 2005)
- *21st Century Super Success* by Chen Anzhi (Knowledge Press, 2001)
- *How to Master the Art of Selling* by Tom Hopkins (Business Plus, 2005)
- *Swim with the Sharks without Being Eaten Alive* by Harvey Mackay (Penguin, 1989)
- *Positioning: The Battle for Your Mind* by Al Ries and Jack Trout (McGraw-Hill, 2000)
- *How to Sell Anything to Anybody* by Joe Girard and Stanley Brown (Fireside, 2006)
- *From the Ground Up* by John P. Coutis (Pan Macmillan, 2001)

About the Author

Dr. Hongman Gao is a doctoral professor in the College of Business at Jackson State University in Mississippi. He earned his PhD in Business Administration from the University of Mississippi. He also holds two master's degrees from the University of Mississippi, one in Computer Science and another in Economics.

Dr. Gao worked at Mississippi's Ashley Furniture, Inc. as a consultant; at Pennsylvania's Beautyman Law Firm as an information systems specialist; at the Department of Finance and the Administration of State-Owned Enterprises as an assistant economist in Zhejiang, China. In addition to teaching at Jackson State University for over two years, Dr. Gao also taught two years at King College in Bristol, Tennessee.

Over the years, Dr. Gao has coauthored books such as *Research in Problems of Chinese Debt* and *Management of Urban Trust Banks*. Dr. Gao also has given research presentations at Tsinghua University, the Graduate School of the People's Bank of China, and Shanghai Jiaotong University. Furthermore, Dr. Gao has published research papers in well-known international journals such as *Expert Systems, International Journal of Production Research, International Journal of Management in Education,* and *International Journal of Service Sciences.*

He is interested in doing consulting projects and is passionate about speaking about investing and attaining success.

You may e-mail Dr. Gao at hongman.gao@hotmail.com.

A Thoughtful Gift

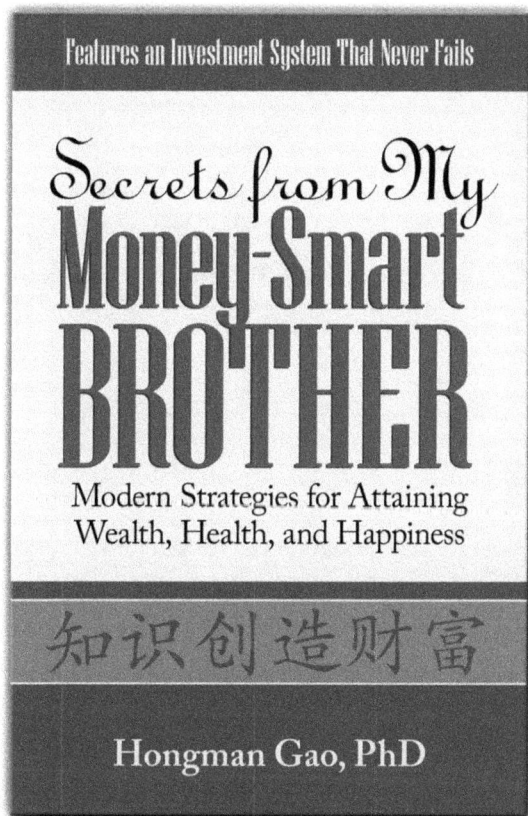

Order *Secrets from My Money Smart Brother:*
Modern Strategies for Attaining Wealth, Health, and Happiness
as a gift for family members and friends.

You can order additional copies
at online book stores such as Amazon.com.

www.ingramcontent.com/pod-product-compliance
Lightning Source LLC
Chambersburg PA
CBHW071946100426

42736CB00042B/2167